DUOLOGUES
FROM THE CLASSICS

LAMDA
DUOLOGUES
FROM THE CLASSICS

Edited by Shaun McKenna

PUBLISHED BY
OBERON BOOKS
FOR THE LONDON ACADEMY OF
MUSIC AND DRAMATIC ART

First published in 2004 for LAMDA Ltd. by Oberon Books Ltd.
(incorporating Absolute Classics)
521 Caledonian Road, London N7 9RH
Tel: 020 7607 3637 / Fax: 020 7607 3629
e-mail: oberon.books@btinternet.com
www.oberonbooks.com

A catalogue record for this book is available from the British Library.

ISBN 1 84002 423 2

Cover design: Joe Ewart

Cover photograph: John Haynes

Printed in Great Britain by Antony Rowe Ltd, Chippenham.

Contents

II: MALE / FEMALE DUOLOGUES

III: FEMALE / FEMALE DUOLOGUES

Introduction

Duologues from the Classics contains duologue scenes for men and women taken from sixteen of the most significant playwrights of the last three millennia. It is a companion volume to the LAMDA/Oberon publication *Monologues from the Classics*.

The scenes have been chosen to be approachable by performers from their mid-teens upwards. Some are clearly more difficult than others and length should not be confused with complexity – some of the shorter scenes are every bit as challenging as the lengthier ones. Playing time ranges from around two-and-a-half minutes to approximately five minutes, though some of the longer scenes can be cut to a variety of lengths depending on the demands of the occasion.

Though the scenes are selected to be suitable for younger actors, this by no means implies that all the characters fall into this age range. Certainly, there is plenty of youthful passion to be found here, but there are also terrific character roles which an adept and ambitious young actor can realistically hope to bring to three-dimensional life. The range of styles is wide, from the bleakest tragedy to the broadest farce and not always from the authors one expects.

One of the pleasures of compiling an anthology of this kind is the discovery (or rediscovery) of great but little-known plays. There are always hundreds of plays that one intends to read 'when there is time'. The list of authors set by LAMDA Examinations for its Advanced Level selections allowed me to explore many forgotten works (amazing the riches that a complete edition of say Wycherley and Behn throws up!) and undisputed masterpieces, to discover the best and most appropriate moments for performance. I felt it was as important to include well-known scenes as it was to unearth less familiar choices. The famous scenes are often famous for good reason and sometimes looking at them in unfamiliar company brings new insights.

In the case of translations, I have given the ISBN of the used version. Editions of English-language plays are readily available.

Restoration period texts have been slightly 'interfered with', it being my belief that the preponderance of capital letters for all nouns is off-putting to the reader. Of the many different editions of Shakespeare, I have chosen to follow the punctuation of the Arden edition. I have provided footnotes where a meaning or reference seems obscure to me, but I hope I have not been over-zealous in providing explanatory notes. The Appendix contains brief biographical details of each of the playwrights. Each scene has a brief introduction outlining the characters and the situation. These will provide useful context when making selections but should not be regarded as a substitute for reading the play.

I hope this collection proves as enjoyable to read as it was to compile.

Shaun McKenna

I: MALE / MALE DUOLOGUES

BACCHAI (406 BC)

by Euripides
Translated by Colin Teevan

PUBLISHED BY OBERON BOOKS (ISBN 1 84002 261 2)

Euripides' last play is a violent tragedy. PENTHEUS, King of Thebes, is arrogant and dismissive of the power of the gods. The god DIONYSUS, disguised as a human, has arrived in Thebes and taught the women of the city to worship him. PENTHEUS is angry and scandalised by the excesses of the god's devotees and demands that DIONYSUS be imprisoned. In interrogating him, PENTHEUS himself falls under the god's spell. Eager to witness the women's rites for himself, PENTHEUS is persuaded by DIONYSUS to disguise himself as a woman. Here, DIONYSUS prepares to lead the disguised PENTHEUS up into the hills.

DIONYSUS: Come Pentheus, time to see what you
should not,
To rush in where you should most fear to tread.
Come out of the house and reveal yourself
Transformed into a Bacchic celebrant.

(*Enter PENTHEUS dressed as a Bacchic woman. He is attended by his Servant.*)

PENTHEUS: I seem to see two suns in the sky
And two cities, two wholly different worlds
One up here in light, in the imagination,
The other –

(*He swoons. DIONYSUS supports him.*)

And you somehow seem to me a bull,
I can now see two horns upon your head.
Were you a bull before? You are one now.
Was I blind before but now see clear?

DIONYSUS: You see things as you should see things.
You have made a deal with Dionysus
And he is with you now.

PENTHEUS: And how do I look? As fair as Ino?
Or even my own mother, Agave?

DIONYSUS: You're the equal of them both in beauty.
But wait, a lock of hair has wriggled free,
Come here and I will slip it back in place.

PENTHEUS: It must have fallen when I was inside,
Dancing up and down and being a Bacchai.

DIONYSUS: Hold still your head and let me fix it.

PENTHEUS: I place myself entirely in your hands.

DIONYSUS: The ribbons on your dress are undone too,
The pleats hang crooked and your slip shows.

PENTHEUS: You're right, I have become a bit undone.
Do everything that needs be done to me.

DIONYSUS: You'll surely count me as a friend for life,
When you see the Bacchai at their play.

PENTHEUS: The stick? The sacred ivy-covered shaft?
Should I hold it in my right hand or the left
To play the part convincingly?

DIONYSUS: The right, and raise your right arm and left foot.
Together. The change in you is striking.

PENTHEUS: I feel as though I had the strength
To bear Mount Cithairon itself upon my back.

DIONYSUS: Now that you're thinking straight, you can
    Do that which you were destined for.

PENTHEUS: Well let us get some crowbars then
    To lever loose the mountain.

DIONYSUS: You'd destroy the home of the mountain
                                 nymphs,
    And the dark woods where Pan plays on his pipes.

PENTHEUS: Yes, you're right, we should not resort to force.
    We shall simply observe them from the pines.

DIONYSUS: But you must choose with utmost care your
                                hiding place,
    Since it's by deceit you choose to watch them.

PENTHEUS: Now that I am changed, I think of them as birds
    Who in their woodland lovenests coo and sigh.

DIONYSUS: Perhaps you'll catch a lovebird or she you?

PENTHEUS: Now lead me through my city's broadest
                              thoroughfares
    For I'm the only man who dares this deed.

DIONYSUS: You alone shall bear your city's burden,
    And you alone shall undergo this trial.
    Now come, I'll lead you to the place,
    Though someone else must bring you home –

PENTHEUS: My mother?

DIONYSUS: The world shall witness your return aloft.

PENTHEUS: Aloft in triumph? Let's go straight there then.

DIONYSUS: Held high by your mother.

PENTHEUS: You're flattering me.

DIONYSUS: The truth.

PENTHEUS: I'll only get what I deserve.

(*Exit PENTHEUS and Servant.*)

DIONYSUS: You're a terrifying man, Pentheus.
And such will be the terror of your end,
Report of it shall spread through all the world.
Agave, daughters or Cadmus, my Bacchai,
Raise up your arms and now receive this man
Whom I deliver to his destiny.
For Dionysus shall prevail,
Though the how and when, only time will tell.

(*DIONYSUS exits.*)

PHILOCTETES (c 405 BC)

by Sophocles
Translated by Keith Dewhurst
PUBLISHED BY OBERON BOOKS (ISBN 1 870259 93 9)

The Trojan war has been going on for ten long years and the Greeks, who are laying siege to Troy, need all the help they can get. The great Greek hero, Achilles, is dead. The wily, cunning general Odysseus has brought Achilles' son, NEOPTOLEMUS, to a deserted island, in order to obtain the magical bow which belongs to PHILOCTETES. PHILOCTETES is an old man, the arch-enemy of Odysseus. He is hideously injured with a wound that never heals, and has become a recluse on this distant island. It is NEOPTOLEMUS' task to use all his powers of persuasion to make PHILOCTETES give up the magic bow – it has been foretold that it will be decisive in assuring a Greek victory. Here, NEOPTOLEMUS has met PHILOCTETES and is trying to get his hands on the bow.

NEOPTOLEMUS: If you're ready we can leave. Why don't you speak? What's happened?

PHILOCTETES: Aaah! Aaah!

NEOPTOLEMUS: What is it?

PHILOCTETES: Nothing to worry about. Go ahead.

NEOPTOLEMUS: D'you feel the pain of your wound?

PHILOCTETES: No. I suddenly feel better. Oh God!

NEOPTOLEMUS: If you're better, why call on God?

PHILOCTETES: To come to me with gentleness, not harm. Ah!

NEOPTOLEMUS: What ails you? Why don't you answer? You're clearly in pain.

PHILOCTETES: Undone, boy! It's beyond my strength to hide it! Aaaah! It stabs me. It goes through me! I'm in agony! I'm finished, boy! Aaaaaaah! Quick! Draw your sword. Cut the end of my foot. Hack it off. Quick! Take my life! Quickly!

NEOPTOLEMUS: What is it, to come on you so suddenly, and make you scream and curse yourself?

PHILOCTETES: You know, boy.

NEOPTOLEMUS: What is it?

PHILOCTETES: You know.

NEOPTOLEMUS: I don't. What is it?

PHILOCTETES: You don't know? Aaaaaaaaah!

NEOPTOLEMUS: This burden of your sickness is terrible.

PHILOCTETES: Terrible beyond words. Pity me.

NEOPTOLEMUS: What must I do?

PHILOCTETES: Don't be afraid or leave me. This comes and after a time goes and in that way drives me out of my senses.

NEOPTOLEMUS: Your suffering's wretched. Shall I hold you?

PHILOCTETES: No. But it is right for you to take the bow and guard it until the pain of my wound passes.

When it does leave me, sleep takes hold, and only that renews me. I need to sleep in peace. If anyone comes here in that time I beg you by the gods not to give up the bow, willing or unwilling. That would kill both of us at the same time.

NEOPTOLEMUS: I'll be brave. Never fear. No-one shall hold it except you and me. Now give it to me.

PHILOCTETES: Here. Receive it, boy. Bow your head to propitiate the jealousy of the gods, lest it becomes the source of sorrow that it was to me and its first owner.

NEOPTOLEMUS: Oh gods, grant us this prayer, and grant us a safe voyage, to where we set our course and you ordain.

PHILOCTETES: Your prayers are empty, boy. Blood gushes from the depths of my wound. I fear a new attack. Ah! It waits for me. Ah! It prowls! It springs near me! Don't leave me! Aaaaah! Oh, if this could run through your chest, Odysseus! Once more. Aah! Agamemnon! Menelaus! May this rot infest your bodies for no less time than mine! Oh! Death, death, how can I call on you always, day after day, and you not come to me? Boy, your blood's honourable, take me to the volcano and summon death from the fire and flames. I had the courage to do it for Heracles the son of Zeus. It's how I won the weapon. Speak! Answer me! Where are you?

NEOPTOLEMUS: In pain like you, but for your griefs.

PHILOCTETES: Stop, boy. Be brave. The pain is quick to come and go. By the same token, don't leave me.

NEOPTOLEMUS: Be brave yourself. We'll wait.

PHILOCTETES: You will?

NEOPTOLEMUS: Be sure.

PHILOCTETES: This is not the place to bind you by oath.

NEOPTOLEMUS: I am bound by honour not to leave you.

PHILOCTETES: Give me your hand on it.

NEOPTOLEMUS: Here.

PHILOCTETES: Then to the other world…

NEOPTOLEMUS: What?

PHILOCTETES: Upwards…

NEOPTOLEMUS: Are you deranged? Why do you stare at the sky?

PHILOCTETES: Let me go.

NEOPTOLEMUS: Where?

PHILOCTETES: Let me go!

NEOPTOLEMUS: Why are you shouting?

PHILOCTETES: Don't kill me! Let me go!

NEOPTOLEMUS: I have let go. You seem more sensible.

PHILOCTETES: Earth, take me. I'm dying. I can't stand upright for the pain.

NEOPTOLEMUS: I think that this man will sleep soon. His head nods. He's covered in sweat and black blood's burst out of his foot like fire. We'll leave him in peace until he falls asleep.

OTHELLO (1604)

by William Shakespeare

IAGO, the apparently honest but deeply manipulative ensign to Othello, governor of Cyprus, has conned RODERIGO, a young nobleman, out of a large amount of money. IAGO has persuaded RODERIGO that Othello's wife, Desdemona, is in love with him. Here, RODERIGO threatens to cut off IAGO's source of income.

Act IV, Scene II

IAGO: How now, Roderigo!

RODERIGO: I do not find that thou dealest justly with me.

IAGO: What in the contrary?

RODERIGO: Every day thou daffest me with some device, Iago; and rather, as it seems to me now, keepest from me all conveniency than suppliest me with the least advantage of hope. I will indeed no longer endure it, nor am I yet persuaded to put up in peace what already I have foolishly suffered.

IAGO: Will you hear me, Roderigo?

RODERIGO: 'Faith, I have heard too much, for your words and performances are no kin together.

IAGO: You charge me most unjustly.

RODERIGO: With nought but truth. I have wasted myself out of my means. The jewels you have had from me to deliver to Desdemona would half have corrupted a votarist: you have told me she hath received them and returned me expectations and comforts of sudden respect and acquaintance, but I find none.

IAGO: Well; go to; very well.

RODERIGO: Very well! go to! I cannot go to, man; nor 'tis not very well: nay, I think it is scurvy, and begin to find myself fobbed in it.

IAGO: Very well.

RODERIGO: I tell you 'tis not very well. I will make myself known to Desdemona: if she will return me my jewels, I will give over my suit and repent my unlawful solicitation; if not, assure yourself I will seek satisfaction of you.

IAGO: You have said now.

RODERIGO: Ay, and said nothing but what I protest intendment of doing.

IAGO: Why, now I see there's mettle in thee, and even from this instant to build on thee a better opinion than ever before. Give me thy hand, Roderigo: thou hast taken against me a most just exception; but yet, I protest, I have dealt most directly in thy affair.

RODERIGO: It hath not appeared.

IAGO: I grant indeed it hath not appeared, and your suspicion is not without wit and judgement. But, Roderigo, if thou hast that in thee indeed, which I have greater reason to believe now than ever, I mean purpose, courage and valour, this night show it: if thou the next night following enjoy not Desdemona, take me from this world with treachery and devise engines for my life.

RODERGIO: Well, what is it? is it within reason and compass?

IAGO: Sir, there is especial commission come from Venice to depute Cassio in Othello's place.

RODERIGO: Is that true? why, then Othello and Desdemona return again to Venice.

IAGO: O, no; he goes into Mauritania and takes away with him the fair Desdemona, unless his abode be lingered here by some accident: wherein none can be so determinate as the removing of Cassio.

RODERIGO: How do you mean, removing of him?

IAGO: Why, by making him uncapable of Othello's place; knocking out his brains.

RODERIGO: And that you would have me to do?

IAGO: Ay, if you dare do yourself a profit and a right. He sups to-night with a harlotry, and thither will I go to him: he knows not yet of his honourable fortune. If you will watch his going thence, which I will fashion to fall out between twelve and one, you may take him at your pleasure: I will be near to second your attempt, and he shall fall between us. Come, stand not amazed at it, but go along with me; I will show you such a necessity in his death that you shall think yourself bound to put it on him. It is now high suppertime, and the night grows to waste: about it.

RODERIGO: I will hear further reason for this.

IAGO: And you shall be satisfied.

(*Exeunt.*)

MEASURE FOR MEASURE (1607)

by William Shakespeare

As a test of the morality of the people of Vienna, DUKE VINCENTIO has allegedly left the city, and put a puritanical leader named Angelo in charge. In fact, the DUKE has disguised himself as a friar and spends his time among the city's low-lifes. LUCIO, a pimp, is here in prison, which the DUKE is visiting.

Act III, Scene II

LUCIO: What news, friar, of the duke?

DUKE VINCENTIO: I know none. Can you tell me of any?

LUCIO: Some say he is with the Emperor of Russia; other some, he is in Rome: but where is he, think you?

DUKE VINCENTIO: I know not where; but wheresoever, I wish him well.

LUCIO: It was a mad fantastical trick of him to steal from the state, and usurp the beggary he was never born to. Lord Angelo dukes it well in his absence; he puts transgression to't.

DUKE VINCENTIO: He does well in't.

LUCIO: A little more lenity to lechery would do no harm in him: something too crabbed that way, friar.

DUKE VINCENTIO: It is too general a vice, and severity must cure it.

LUCIO: Yes, in good sooth, the vice is of a great kindred; it is well allied: but it is impossible to extirp it quite, friar, till eating and drinking be put down. They say this Angelo was not made by man and woman after this downright way of creation: is it true, think you?

DUKE VINCENTIO: How should he be made, then?

LUCIO: Some report a sea-maid spawned him; some, that he was begot between two stock-fishes. But it is certain that when he makes water his urine is congealed ice; that I know to be true: and he is a motion generative; that's infallible.

DUKE VINCENTIO: You are pleasant, sir, and speak apace.

LUCIO: Why, what a ruthless thing is this in him, for the rebellion of a codpiece to take away the life of a man! Would the duke that is absent have done this? Ere he would have hanged a man for the getting a hundred bastards, he would have paid for the nursing a thousand: he had some feeling of the sport: he knew the service, and that instructed him to mercy.

DUKE VINCENTIO: I never heard the absent duke much detected for women; he was not inclined that way.

LUCIO: O, sir, you are deceived.

DUKE VINCENTIO: 'Tis not possible.

LUCIO: Who, not the duke? yes, your beggar of fifty; and his use was to put a ducat in her clack-dish: the duke had crotchets in him. He would be drunk too; that let me inform you.

DUKE VINCENTIO: You do him wrong, surely.

LUCIO: Sir, I was an inward of his. A shy fellow was the duke: and I believe I know the cause of his withdrawing.

DUKE VINCENTIO: What, I prithee, might be the cause?

LUCIO: No, pardon; 'tis a secret must be locked within the teeth and the lips: but this I can let you understand, the greater file of the subject held the duke to be wise.

DUKE VINCENTIO: Wise! why, no question but he was.

LUCIO: A very superficial, ignorant, unweighing fellow.

DUKE VINCENTIO: Either this is the envy in you, folly, or mistaking: the very stream of his life and the business he hath helmed must upon a warranted need give him a better proclamation. Let him be but testimonied in his own bringings-forth, and he shall appear to the envious a scholar, a statesman and a soldier. Therefore you speak unskilfully: or if your knowledge be more it is much darkened in your malice.

LUCIO: Sir, I know him, and I love him.

DUKE VINCENTIO: Love talks with better knowledge, and knowledge with dearer love.

LUCIO: Come, sir, I know what I know.

DUKE VINCENTIO: I can hardly believe that, since you know not what you speak. But, if ever the duke return, as our prayers are he may, let me desire you to make your answer before him. If it be honest you have spoke, you have courage to maintain it: I am bound to call upon you; and, I pray you, your name?

LUCIO: Sir, my name is Lucio; well known to the duke.

DUKE VINCENTIO: He shall know you better, sir, if I may live to report you.

LUCIO: I fear you not.

THE DUCHESS OF MALFI (1614)

by John Webster

FERDINAND, Duke of Calabria, is the brother of both the CARDINAL and the widowed Duchess of the title. FERDINAND has an incestuous passion for his sister and is fiercely jealous of her reputation – so much so that, when she falls in love with her steward, Antonio, she is forced to marry him in secret. Here, FERDINAND and his brother, the corrupt CARDINAL, have heard rumours about the Duchess's marriage.

Act II, Scene V

Enter CARDINAL, and FERDINAND with a letter.

FERDINAND: I have this night digg'd up a mandrake.[1]

CARDINAL: Say you?

FERDINAND: And I am grown mad with't.

CARDINAL: What's the prodigy?

FERDINAND: Read there, a sister damn'd: she's loose
                                                i'th'hilts;
   Grown a notorious strumpet.

CARDINAL: Speak lower.

FERDINAND: Lower!
   Rogues do not whisper't now, but seek to publish't
   (As servants do the bounty of their lords)
   Aloud; and with a covetous searching eye,
   To mark who note them. O, confusion seize her!
   She hath had most cunning bawds to serve her turn,

1 *mandrake* plant used in witchcraft

And more secure conveyances for lust,
Than towns of garrison for service.

CARDINAL: Is't possible?
Can this be certain?

FERDINAND: Rhubarb, O, for rhubarb,
To purge this choler![2] Here's the cursed day
To prompt my memory; and here't shall stick
Till of her bleeding heart I make a sponge
To wipe it out.

CARDINAL: Why do you make yourself
So wild a tempest?

FERDINAND: Would I could be one,
That I might toss her palace 'bout her ears,
Root up her goodly forests, blast her meads[3],
And lay her general territory as waste,
As she hath done her honours.

CARDINAL: Shall our blood,
The royal blood of Arragon and Castile,
Be thus attainted?

FERDINAND: Apply desperate physic:
We must not now use balsamum[4], but fire,
The smarting cupping-glass, for that's the mean
To purge infected blood, such blood as hers.
There is a kind of pity in mine eye,
I'll give it to my handkerchief; and now 'tis here
I'll bequeath this to her bastard.

CARDINAL: What to do?

2 *choler* sickness. Rhubarb was used as a purgative
3 *meads* meadows
4 *balsamum etc* references to contemporary purging medicine

FERDINAND: Why, to make soft lint for his mother's
                                                wounds,
   When I have hewed her to pieces.

CARDINAL: Curs'd creature!
   Unequal nature, to place women's hearts
   So far upon the left side!

FERDINAND: Foolish men,
   That e'er will trust their honour in a bark[5]
   Made of so slight weak bulrush as is woman,
   Apt every minute to sink it!

CARDINAL: Thus
   Ignorance, when it hath purchas'd honour,
   It cannot wield it.

FERDINAND: Methinks I see her laughing: –
   Excellent hyena! Talk to me somewhat, quickly,
   Or my imagination will carry me
   To see her in the shameful act of sin.

CARDINAL: With whom?

FERDINAND: Happily with some strong-thigh'd
                                                bargeman,
   Or one o'th' wood-yard, that can quoit the sledge,
   Or toss the bar, or else some lovely squire
   That carries coals up to her privy lodgings.

CARDINAL: You fly beyond your reason.

FERDINAND: Go to, mistress!
   'Tis not your whore's milk that shall quench my wild-fire,
   But your whore's blood.

CARDINAL: How idly shews this rage, which carries you,
   As men convey'd by witches through the air,

5 *bark* boat

On violent whirlwinds! this intemperate noise
Fitly resembles deaf men's shrill discourse,
Who talk aloud, thinking all other men
To have their imperfection.

FERDINAND: Have not you
My palsy?

CARDINAL: Yes; I can be angry
Without this rupture: there is not in nature
A thing that makes man so deform'd, so beastly,
As doth intemperate anger. Chide yourself.
You have divers men, who never yet express'd
Their strong desire of rest, but by unrest,
By vexing of themselves. Come, put yourself
In tune.

FERDINAND: So: I will not only study to seem
The thing I am not. I could kill her now,
In you, or in myself; for I do think
It is some sin in us, heaven doth revenge
By her.

CARDINAL: Are you stark mad?

FERDINAND: I would have their
                                   bodies
Burnt in a coal-pit with the ventage stopp'd,
That their curs'd smoke might not ascend to heaven;
Or dip the sheets they lie in in pitch or sulphur,
Wrap them in't, and then light them like a match;
Or else to boil their bastard to a cullis
And give't his lecherous father, to renew
The sin of his back.

CARDINAL: I'll leave you.

FERDINAND: Nay, I have done.
  I am confident, had I been damn'd in hell,
  And should have heard of this, it would have put me
  Into a cold sweat. In, in, I'll go sleep.
  Till I know who leaps my sister, I'll not stir:
  That known, I'll find scorpions to string my whips,
  And fix her in a general eclipse.

  (*Exeunt.*)

THE OLD BACHELOR (1693)

by William Congreve

In this, the opening scene of the play, we meet two young men about town, both interested in two things – women and money. VAINLOVE is the more fickle, flighty and cynical of the pair, while BELLMOUR is handsome and much in demand from ladies. The scene is a fashionable London street.

Act I, Scene I

BELLMOUR and VAINLOVE meeting.

BELLMOUR: Vainlove, and abroad so early! Good-morrow; I thought a contemplative lover could no more have parted with his bed in a morning than he could have slept in't.

VAINLOVE: Bellmour, good-morrow. Why, truth on't is, these early sallies are not usual to me; but business, as you see, sir – (*Showing letters.*) And business must be followed, or be lost.

BELLMOUR: Business! And so must time, my friend, be close pursued, or lost. Business is the rub of life, perverts our aim, casts off the bias, and leaves us wide and short of the intended mark.

VAINLOVE: Pleasure, I guess you mean.

BELLMOUR: Ay; what else has meaning?

VAINLOVE: Oh, the wise will tell you –

BELLMOUR: More than they believe – or understand.

VAINLOVE: How, how, Ned! A wise man say more than he understands?

BELLMOUR: Ay, ay! Wisdom's nothing but a pretending to know and believe more than we really do. You read of but one wise man, and all that he knew was, that he knew nothing. Come, come, leave business to idlers and wisdom to fools; they have need of 'em. Wit be my faculty, and pleasure my occupation; and let Father Time shake his glass. Let low and earthly souls grovel till they have worked themselves six foot deep into a grave. Business is not my element – I roll in a higher orb, and dwell –

VAINLOVE: In castles i' th' air of thy own building. That's thy element, Ned. Well, as high a flier as you are, I have a lure may make you stoop. (*Flings a letter.*)

BELLMOUR: I, marry, sir, I have a hawk's eye at a woman's hand. There's more elegancy in the false spelling of this superscription (*Takes up the letter.*) than in all Cicero. Let me see – How now! (*Reads.*) Dear PERFIDIOUS VAINLOVE.

VAINLOVE: Hold, hold, 'slife, that's the wrong one.

BELLMOUR: Nay, let's see the name – Sylvia! – how canst thou be ungrateful to that creature? She's extremely pretty, and loves thee entirely – I have heard her breathe such raptures about thee –

VAINLOVE: Ay, or anybody that she's about –

BELLMOUR: No, faith, Frank, you wrong her; she has been just to you.

VAINLOVE: That's pleasant, by my troth, from thee, who hast had her.

BELLMOUR: Never – her affections. 'Tis true, by heaven: she owned it to my face; and, blushing like the virgin morn when it disclosed the cheat which that trusty bawd of nature, night, had hid, confessed her soul was true to you; though I by treachery had stolen the bliss.

VAINLOVE: So was true as turtle – in imagination – Ned, ha? Preach this doctrine to husbands, and the married women will adore thee.

BELLMOUR: Why, faith, I think it will do well enough, if the husband be out of the way, for the wife to show her fondness and impatience of his absence by choosing a lover as like him as she can; and what is unlike, she may help out with her own fancy.

VAINLOVE: But is it not an abuse to the lover to be made a blind of?

BELLMOUR: As you say, the abuse is to the lover, not the husband. For 'tis an argument of her great zeal towards him, that she will enjoy him in effigy.

VAINLOVE: It must be a very superstitious country where such zeal passes for true devotion. I doubt it will be damned by all our Protestant husbands for flat idolatry. But, if you can make Alderman Fondlewife of your persuasion, this letter will be needless.

BELLMOUR: What! The old banker with the handsome wife?

VAINLOVE: Ay.

BELLMOUR: Let me see – LAETITIA! Oh, 'tis a delicious morsel. Dear Frank, thou art the truest friend in the world.

VAINLOVE: Ay, am I not? To be continually starting of hares for you to course. We were certainly cut out for one another; for my temper quits an amour just where thine takes it up. But read that; it is an appointment for me, this evening – when Fondlewife will be gone out of town, to meet the master of a ship, about the return of a venture which he's in danger of losing. Read, read.

BELLMOUR: (*Reads.*) Hum, Hum – Out of town this evening, and talks of sending for Mr Spintext to keep me company; but I'll take care he shall not be at home. Good! Spintext! Oh, the fanatic one-eyed parson!

VAINLOVE: Ay.

BELLMOUR: (*Reads.*) Hum, Hum – That your conversation will be much more agreeable, if you can counterfeit his habit to blind the servants. Very good! Then I must be disguised? – With all my heart! – It adds a gusto to an amour; gives it the greater resemblance of theft; and, among us lewd mortals, the deeper the sin the sweeter. Frank, I'm amazed at thy good nature –

VAINLOVE: Faith, I hate love when 'tis forced upon a man, as I do wine. And this business is none of my seeking; I only happened to be, once or twice, where Laetitia was the handsomest woman in company; so, consequently, applied myself to her – and it seems she has taken me at my word. Had you been there, or anybody, 't had been the same.

BELLMOUR: I wish I may succeed as the same.

VAINLOVE: Never doubt it; for if the spirit of cuckoldom be once raised up in a woman, the devil can't lay it, until she has done't.

LOVE FOR LOVE (1695)

by William Congreve

VALENTINE is a young man who has quickly run through his inheritance, living as a man of fashion. Now he finds himself in debt with no means of helping his situation, except by marriage, a course he is unwilling to pursue. So he decides to turn to writing instead, as a means of making his living. JEREMY is his servant and friend.

Act I, Scene I

VALENTINE in his chamber reading. JEREMY waiting. Several books upon the table.

VALENTINE: Jeremy.

JEREMY: Sir?

VALENTINE: Here, take away. I'll walk a turn and digest what I have read.

JEREMY: (*Aside, and taking away the books.*) You'll grow devilish fat upon this paper diet.

VALENTINE: And d'ye hear, go you to breakfast. There's a page doubled down in Epictetus, that is a feast for an emperor.

JEREMY: Was Epictetus a real cook, or did he only write receipts?

VALENTINE: Read, read, sirrah, and refine your appetite; learn to live upon instruction; feast your mind and mortify your flesh; read, and take your nourishment in at your eyes; shut up your mouth, and chew the cud of understanding. So Epictetus advises.

JEREMY: O Lord! I have heard much of him, when I waited upon a gentleman at Cambridge. Pray what was that Epictetus?

VALENTINE: A very rich man. – Not worth a groat.

JEREMY: Humph, and so he has made a very fine feast, where there is nothing to be eaten?

VALENTINE: Yes.

JEREMY: Sir, you're a gentleman, and probably understand this fine feeding: but if you please, I had rather be at board wages. Does your Epictetus, or your Seneca here, or any of these poor rich rogues, teach you how to pay your debts without money? Will they shut up the mouths of your creditors? Will Plato be bail for you? Or Diogenes, because he understands confinement, and lived in a tub, go to prison for you? 'Slife, sir, what do you mean, to mew yourself up here with three or four musty books, in commendation of starving and poverty?

VALENTINE: Why, sirrah, I have no money, you know it; and therefore resolve to rail at all that have. And in that I but follow the examples of the wisest and wittiest men in all ages, these poets and philosophers whom you naturally hate, for just such another reason; because they abound in sense, and you are a fool.

JEREMY: Ay, sir, I am a fool, I know it: and yet, heaven help me, I'm poor enough to be a wit. But I was always a fool when I told you what your expenses would bring you to; your coaches and your liveries;

your treats and your balls; your being in love with a lady that did not care a farthing for you in your prosperity; and keeping company with wits that cared for nothing but your prosperity; and now, when you are poor, hate you as much as they do one another.

VALENTINE: Well, and now I am poor I have an opportunity to be revenged on them all. I'll pursue Angelica with more love than ever, and appear more notoriously her admirer in this restraint, than when I openly rivalled the rich fops that made court to her. So shall my poverty be a mortification to her pride, and, perhaps, make her compassionate the love which has principally reduced me to this lowness of fortune. And for the wits, I'm sure I am in a condition to be even with them.

JEREMY: Nay, your condition is pretty even with theirs, that's the truth on't.

VALENTINE: I'll take some of their trade out of their hands.

JEREMY: Now heaven of mercy continue the tax upon paper. You don't mean to write?

VALENTINE: Yes, I do. I'll write a play.

JEREMY: Hem! Sir, if you please to give me a small certificate of three lines – only to certify those whom it may concern, that the bearer hereof, Jeremy Fetch by name, has for the space of seven years truly and faithfully served Valentine Legend, Esq., and that he is not now turned away for any misdemeanour, but does voluntarily dismiss his master from any future authority over him –

VALENTINE: No, sirrah; you shall live with me still.

JEREMY: Sir, it's impossible. I may die with you, starve with you, or be damned with your works. But to live, even three days, the life of a play, I no more expect it than to be canonized for a muse after my decease.

VALENTINE: You are witty, you rogue. I shall want your help. I'll have you learn to make couplets to tag the ends of acts. D'ye hear? Get the maids to Crambo in an evening, and learn the knack of rhyming: you may arrive at the height of a song sent by an unknown hand, or a chocolate-house lampoon.

JEREMY: But, sir, is this the way to recover your father's favour? Why, Sir Sampson will be irreconcilable. If your younger brother should come from sea, he'd never look upon you again. You're undone, sir; you're ruined; you won't have a friend left in the world if you turn poet.

THE RECRUITING OFFICER (1706)

by George Farquhar

PLUME, the Recruiting Officer of the title, is in Shrewsbury to raise soldiers for the army. He has sent his sergeant, the street-wise and wily KITE, ahead of him. Here, PLUME has just arrived in town after a long ride from London.

Act I, Scene I

PLUME: By the grenadier-march that shou'd be my drum, and by that shout it shou'd beat with success – Let me see. (*Looks on his Watch.*) Four o'clock – At ten yesterday morning I left London – A hundred and twenty miles in thirty hours, is pretty smart riding, but nothing to the fatigue of recruiting.

(*Enter KITE.*)

KITE: Welcome to Shrewsbury, noble Captain, from the banks of the Danube to the Severn side, noble Captain you are welcome.

PLUME: A very elegant reception indeed, Mr Kite, I find you are fairly enter'd into your recruiting strain – Pray what success?

KITE: I have been here but a week, and I have recruited five.

PLUME: Five! Pray, what are they?

KITE: I have listed the strong man of Kent, the King of the Gypsies, a scowling pedlar, a scoundrel attorney, and a Welsh parson.

PLUME: An attorney! Wer't thou mad? List a lawyer!
   Discharge him, discharge him this minute.

KITE: Why sir?

PLUME: Because I will have nobody in my company that
   can write; a fellow that can write, can draw petitions –
   I say, this minute discharge him.

KITE: And what shall I do with the parson?

PLUME: Can he write?

KITE: Umh – He plays rarely upon the fiddle.

PLUME: Keep him by all means – But how stands the
   country affected? Were the people pleas'd with the
   news of my coming to town?

KITE: Sir, the mob are so pleas'd with your Honour, and
   the Justices and better sort of people are so delighted
   with me, that we shall soon do our business – But, Sir,
   you have got a recruit here that you little think of.

PLUME: Who?

KITE: One that you beat up for last time you were in the
   country; you remember your old friend Molly at the
   castle.

PLUME: She's not with child, I hope.

KITE: No, no, Sir; – She was brought to bed yesterday.

PLUME: Kite, you must father the child.

KITE: Humph – And so her friends will oblige me to
   marry the mother.

PLUME: If they shou'd, we'll take her with us, she can
   wash you know, and make a bed upon occasion.

KITE: Ay, or unmake it upon occasion, but your Honour knows that I'm marry'd already.

PLUME: Tohowmany?

KITE: I can't tell readily – I have set them down here upon the back of the muster-roll. (*Draws out the Muster-Roll*) Let me see. Imprimis, Mrs Sally Snickle-eyes, she sells potatoes upon Ormond-Key in Dublin – Peggy Guzzle, the brandy woman at the Horse-Guard at Whitehall – Dolly Waggon, the carrier's daughter in Hull – Mademoseille Van-Bottomflat at the Buss – Then Jenny Okam the ship-carpenter's widow at Portsmouth; but I don't reckon upon her, for she was marry'd at the same time to two Lieutenants of Marines, and a Man of War's boatswain.

PLUME: A full company, you have nam'd five. Come, make 'em half a dozen, Kite – Is the child a boy or a girl?

KITE: A chopping boy.

PLUME: Then set the mother down in your list, and the boy in mine; enter him a grenadier by the name of Francis Kite, absent upon furlow – I'll allow you a man's pay for his subsistence, and now go comfort the wench in the straw.

KITE: I shall, Sir.

PLUME: But hold, have you made any use of your German doctor's habit since you arriv'd?

KITE: Yes, yes, Sir; and my fame's all about the country, for the most famous fortune-teller that ever told a lie; I was oblig'd to let my landlord into the secret for the convenience of keeping it so; but he's an honest fellow, and will be trusty to any roguery that is confided to him: This device, Sir, will get you men, and me money, which I think is all we want at present – But yonder comes your friend, Mr Worthy – Has your Honour any farther commands?

PLUME: None at present.

(*Exit KITE.*)

'Tis indeed the picture of Worthy, but the life's departed.

THE BEAUX STRATEGEM (1707)

by George Farquhar

AIMWELL and ARCHER are a pair of impoverished noblemen who have gone through their respective fortunes. They have devised a scheme whereby one pretends to be the servant of the other, in order to live well and make a living. They have arrived at an inn in Lichfield and a new adventure is about to begin.

Act I, Scene I

AIMWELL: The coast's clear, I see – Now my dear Archer, welcome to Lichfield.

ARCHER: I thank thee, my dear brother in iniquity.

AIMWELL: Iniquity! Prithee leave canting, you need not change your style with your dress.

ARCHER: Don't mistake me, Aimwell, for 'tis still my maxim, that there is no scandal like rags, nor any crime so shameful as poverty.

AIMWELL: The world confesses it every day in its practice, tho' men won't own it for their opinion. Who did that worthy lord, my brother, single out of the side-box to sup with him t'other night?

ARCHER: Jack Handycraft, a handsome, well dress'd, mannerly, sharping rogue who keeps the best company in town.

AIMWELL: Right, and pray who marry'd my Lady Manslaughter t'other day, the great fortune?

ARCHER: Why, Wick Marrabone, a profess'd pick-pocket, and a good bowler; but he makes a handsome figure, and rides in his coach, that he formerly used to ride behind.

AIMWELL: But did you observe poor Jack Generous in the park last week?

ARCHER: Yes, with his autumnal periwig, shading his melancholy face, his coat older than any thing but its fashion, with one hand idle in his pocket, and with the other picking his useless teeth; and tho' the Mall was crowded with company, yet was poor Jack as single and solitary as a lion in a desert.

AIMWELL: And as much avoided, for no crime upon earth but the want of money.

ARCHER: And that's enough; Men must not be poor, idleness is the root of all evil; the world's wide enough, let 'em bustle; Fortune has taken the weak under her protection, but men of sense are left to their industry.

AIMWELL: Upon which topic we proceed, and I think luckily hitherto: Wou'd not any man swear now that I am a man of quality, and you my servant, when if our intrinsic value were known –

ARCHER: Come, come, we are men of intrinsic value, who can strike our fortunes out of our selves, whose worth is independent of accidents in life, or revolutions in government; we have heads to get money, and hearts to spend it.

AIMWELL: As to our hearts, I grant ye, they are as willing tits as any within twenty degrees; but I can have no great opinion of our heads from the service they have done us hitherto, unless it be that they have brought us from London hither to Lichfield, made me a lord, and you my servant.

ARCHER: That's more than you cou'd expect already. But what money have we left?

AIMWELL: But two hundred pound.

ARCHER: And our horses, clothes, rings, etc. Why, we have very good fortunes now for moderate people; and let me tell you, besides, that this two hundred pound, with the experience that we are now masters of, is a better estate than the ten thousand we have spent. – Our friends indeed began to suspect that our pockets were low but we came off with flying colours, shew'd no signs of want either in word or deed.

AIMWELL: Ay, and our going to Brussels was a good pretence enough for our sudden disappearing; and I warrant you, our friends imagine that we are gone a volunteering.

ARCHER: Why, faith, if this prospect fails, it must e'en come to that, I am for venturing one of the hundreds if you will upon this knight-errantry. But in case it should fail, we'll reserve the t'other to carry us to some counterscarp, where we may die as we liv'd – in a blaze.

AIMWELL: With all my heart; and we have liv'd justly, Archer, we can't say that we have spent our fortunes, but that we have enjoy'd 'em.

ARCHER: Right, so much pleasure for so much money, we have had our pennyworths, and had I millions, I wou'd go to the same market again. O London, London! Well, we have had our share, and let us be thankful; past pleasures, for aught I know, are best, such as we are sure of. Those to come may disappoint us.

AIMWELL: It has often griev'd the heart of me, to see how some inhumane wretches murder their kind fortunes; those that by sacrificing all to one appetite, shall starve all the rest. – You shall have some that live only in their palates, and in their sense of tasting shall drown the other four: Others are only epicures in appearances, such who shall starve their nights to make a figure a days, and famish their own to feed the eyes of others: A contrary sort confine their pleasures to the dark, and contract their spacious acres to the circuit of a muff-string.

ARCHER: Right; but they find the Indies in that spot where they consume 'em, and I think your kind keepers have much the best on't; for they indulge the most senses by one expense, there's the seeing, hearing, and feeling amply gratify'd; and some philosophers will tell you, that from such a commerce there arises a sixth sense that gives infinitely more pleasure than the other five put together.

AIMWELL: And to pass to the other extremity, of all keepers, I think those the worst that keep their money.

ARCHER: Those are the most miserable wights in being, they destroy the rights of Nature, and disappoint the blessings of Providence: Give me a man that keeps his five senses keen and bright as his sword, that has 'em always drawn out in their just order and strength, with his reason as commander at the head of 'em, that detaches 'em by turns upon whatever party of pleasure agreeably offers, and commands 'em to retreat upon the least appearance of disadvantage or danger:– For my part I can stick to my bottle, while my wine, my company, and my reason holds good; I can be charm'd with Sappho's singing without falling in love with her face; I love hunting, but wou'd not, like Acteon, be eaten up by my own dogs; I love a fine house, but let another keep it; and just so I love a fine woman.

AIMWELL: In that last particular you have the better of me.

ARCHER: Ay, you're such an amorous puppy, that I'm afraid you'll spoil our sport; you can't counterfeit the passion without feeling it.

AIMWELL: Tho' the whining part be out of doors in town, 'tis still in force with the country ladies; – And let me tell you, Frank, the fool in that passion shall outdo the knave at any time.

ARCHER: Well, I won't dispute it now, you command for the day, and so I submit; – At Nottingham you know I am to be master.

AIMWELL: And at Lincoln I again.

ARCHER: Then at Norwich I mount, which, I think, shall be our last stage; for if we fail there, we'll embark for Holland, bid adieu to Venus, and welcome Mars.

AIMWELL: A Match!

FRIENDS AND LOVERS (1751)

by Carlo Goldoni

Translated by Robert David MacDonald

PUBLISHED BY OBERON BOOKS (ISBN 1 870259 37 8)

Goldoni's comedy is set in Hamburg in the neighbouring apartments of SEBASTIAN and Herr Mayer. The plot turns on misplaced and misunderstood letters, the resulting confusions spiralling into farce. FLORINDO has been staying with his friend, SEBASTIAN. SEBASTIAN is in love with his neighbour's daughter, Clara. FLORINDO has decided to leave Hamburg because he too has fallen in love with Clara. Here FLORINDO tries to explain his reasons for leaving.

Act I, Scene I

FLORINDO: It will be a token of your friendship if you will let me go without further attempts to prevent me.

SEBASTIAN: If that is what you want. Do me one favour though.

FLORINDO: Well?

SEBASTIAN: Wait until tomorrow.

FLORINDO: I should rather leave today.

SEBASTIAN: No, tomorrow. Today I need you.

FLORINDO: For what?

SEBASTIAN: You know I am engaged to marry Clara? Well, you do know, don't you?

FLORINDO: Yes. I know.

SEBASTIAN: You also know the shaky condition of our family finances. I hope to set all to rights with Clara's dowry; 20,000 marks her father has promised. But apart from that, she is a girl of great beauty and grace. Well, don't you agree? Is she not particularly fine? Intelligent? What is the matter? Don't you approve of her? Don't you find her beautiful?

FLORINDO: Yes. She is. Beautiful.

SEBASTIAN: She seemed to be in love with me, and for a while, I thought she was satisfied with me. But for some time now she has changed towards me, she no longer speaks so warmly, indeed she treats me with considerable coolness. I have tried to force the cause of this from her, but to no avail. I have gone so far as to suggest that if she has repented of our engagement, we are still in time to tear up the contract.

FLORINDO: What did she say to that?

SEBASTIAN: That the marriage had been arranged by her father, that she had no authority to cancel it, and that if it was I that was dissatisfied, then I should say so.

FLORINDO: That sounds like a modest well brought-up girl.

SEBASTIAN: Exactly, a modest well brought-up girl who does not love me.

FLORINDO: Oh, come now, it just seems like that to you. Women are subject to these minor vagaries just like anyone else.

SEBASTIAN: Women are changeable.

FLORINDO: And what about the rest of us? Have you never found yourself in her presence and with no desire to speak to her? Why should you imagine a girl always has to be of one mind? Would you wish her to laugh when she does not feel like doing so?

SEBASTIAN: Well, then, you go to see her. Bring the talk round to me…

FLORINDO: Sebastian, please – reckon without me in this. I have no wish to see the Signora Clara.

SEBASTIAN: What is this? Are you going to leave without taking farewell of a house where you have been received in conversation every day? Clara's father is your friend.

FLORINDO: I really have a great deal to see to; I beg you to make my farewells for me.

SEBASTIAN: But if you're not leaving till tomorrow, you can make them yourself.

FLORINDO: No. I must leave at once.

SEBASTIAN: You promised.

FLORINDO: Then I shall stay here with you, but I have no wish to socialise.

SEBASTIAN: Is there some mystery makes you unwilling to see Clara?

FLORINDO: What the devil do you mean? I am a man of honour…

SEBASTIAN: I meant you might have received some slight from her father. Squalid old miser, he would not hesitate to slight a friend for the meanest economy.

FLORINDO: Perhaps, but he is an old man, he has nothing in the world but his daughter, and if he makes economies, he makes them for you.

SEBASTIAN: But if he has put some slight upon you, I want to know. I should take it as a personal affront.

FLORINDO: No, no, he has done nothing.

SEBASTIAN: Then let us go and visit him.

FLORINDO: No, please, if you love me…

SEBASTIAN: Then it is Clara who has displeased you.

FLORINDO: She is incapable of displeasing anyone.

SEBASTIAN: Then you can have no reason to refuse. Come on.

FLORINDO: No, Sebastian…

SEBASTION: Friend, if you go on refusing me, I shall begin to suspect something worse. What is your answer?

FLORINDO: I do not wish to discuss it now. I will go wherever you wish.

SEBASTIAN: Let us go then. I want you to use your skill to raise Clara's spirits: bring the conversation round to me, and, if she has formed some bad impression of me, try to disabuse her. But if she has decided not to love me, I would like you to say, on my behalf, that a person who does not love me, does not deserve me.

FLORINDO: I am not good at that sort of thing.

SEBASTIAN: I know how expert you are in such situations. I have no friend I can trust as I do you. You owe me this favour before leaving: I can't believe you would want to leave me thinking you were no longer my friend.

FLORINDO: Whatever you wish.

SEBASTIAN: I shall go up with you, then leave you to your discussion. I expect you to bring me comfort and counsel. According to your report of her, I shall either leave off loving her altogether, or hasten on my marriage.

THE VENETIAN TWINS (1748)

by Carlo Goldoni
Translated by Ranjit Bolt

PUBLISHED BY OBERON BOOKS (ISBN 0 948230 63 0)

PANCRAZIO is in love with Rosaura, the daughter of Dr Balanzoni. Dr Balanzoni has arranged for Rosaura to marry the handsome but boorish Venetian, Zanetto. However, Zanetto has a charming, gentlemanly twin brother, TONINO. When TONINO arrives in town on the same day as Zanetto, mistaken identities cause farcical twists in this robust comedy – which is reminiscent of The Comedy of Errors. In this scene, PANCRAZIO believes TONINO to be Zanetto.

Act II, Scene XII

PANCRAZIO: My respects, signor Zanetto.

TONINO: Your servant.

PANCRAZIO: Your excellency, I'm sorry for you. It seems you have not followed my advice.

TONINO: On the contrary, you look like the sort of man whose advice one should always follow.

PANCRAZIO: And then… (*Breaks off.*) Forgive me for mentioning it, but your accent – it seems – how can I put this? – rather less plebeian than when we last spoke.

TONINO: You're not the first person who's said that to me today.

PANCRAZIO: However, to continue – I was under the

impression that you had taken what I said to heart –
and now I find you here.

TONINO: (*Aside.*) Let's see what I can find out.
(*Aloud.*) There are some evil people in this house.

PANCRAZIO: Too true.

TONINO: Grasping people.

PANCRAZIO: I do so agree.

TONINO: This doctor, for example. He's a scoundrel.

PANCRAZIO: You are clearly a most perceptive man –
you've seen through him already.

TONINO: And the girl?

PANCRAZIO: Not to be trusted.

TONINO: But she's so beautiful.

PANCRAZIO: Appearances can be deceptive.

TONINO: So what are you doing here, with all these
wicked people?

PANCRAZIO: I consider it my duty to reform them. I do
my best to enlighten them – to make them change
their ways. But thus far, my seeds of wisdom have
fallen on stony ground.

TONINO: You can't build with rotten wood. All the
same, one can't help liking the girl.

PANCRAZIO: She could melt a heart of stone. I pity the
man who falls for it.

TONINO: She tried to trap me into marriage.

PANCRAZIO: Not marriage! Please – not that vile word again!

TONINO: Vile? I don't know what you mean.

PANCRAZIO: But, my dear signor Zanetto, surely you remember: a burden that makes you sweat by day and keeps you awake at night; a burden on the body and on the mind?

TONINO: Rubbish! A burden on the mind? On the contrary, a wife can relieve your anxiety. She looks after the finances and the servants. With that natural feminine cunning, which some people call avarice, she may even – at the end of the year – make profits for the household. You know what the Venetian poet says:
'You'll marry if you've got a brain
And aren't averse to compromise.
Those who oppose what I advise
Are impotent or else insane.'

PANCRAZIO: (*Aside.*) This fellow's not the fool I took him for! (*Aloud.*) But have you forgotten that a woman is a siren who will lure you to destruction? That she will flatter you to deceive and plunge you into penury?

TONINO: Nonsense. What about the frog and the nightingale? A frog is sitting in a ditch with his mouth wide open. A nightingale sees his throat and falls in love with it. She circles him for a while, then dives straight in. He eats her. Whose fault is it – the nightingale's, or the frog's?

PANCRAZIO: (*Aside.*) He's far too good for me! What am I going to do? (*Aloud.*) I don't know what to say. If you want her, take her. But I beg of you – for your own sake – don't do anything rash.

TONINO: I didn't say I wanted her. I may have defended marriage, but that doesn't mean I want to get married. She's neither fish nor fowl. And you've made me even more suspicious. I think I'll just drop the whole thing.

PANCRAZIO: Excellent! Well said! I heartily approve of your decision.

TONINO: You seem trustworthy. I'll let you into a secret.

PANCRAZIO: I can assure you, it will be safe with me.

TONINO: You see this box of jewels.

PANCRAZIO: Jewels!

TONINO: That's right.

PANCRAZIO: Let me see them. (*Examines them.*) Beautiful! Really beautiful!

TONINO: They were given to me by a lunatic in a shabby coat. I don't know who they belong to, but he must be frantic by now. I wonder if I could leave them with you – in case he turns up.

PANCRAZIO: You are indeed an honourable man.

TONINO: I'm only acting as a gentleman should.

PANCRAZIO: But if – after a diligent search, of course – the owner cannot be found…?

TONINO: Give them as dowries to young brides.

PANCRAZIO: You Venetians have hearts of gold.

TONINO: Lots of people depend on gentlemen like me. Some of us exploit the situation. Others, of whom I am one, act from purely selfless motives. I'd give all I've got for a friend – even the shirt off my back. (*Goes.*)

PANCRAZIO: What an incredible stroke of luck! It seems he's not so clever after all. I shall use his charity to soothe my own ills. If Rosaura wants these jewels, she'll have to pay with the sort of currency that doesn't cost her much, but means a great deal to me. (*Goes.*)

THE RIVALS (1775)

by Richard Brinsley Sheridan

In the opening scene of the play, two servants from the household of Sir Anthony Absolute meet in a fashionable street in Bath and catch up with one another's news. THOMAS is a coachman and FAG the manservant of Captain Jack Absolute, Sir Anthony's son.

Act I, Scene I

Enter THOMAS; he crosses the stage; FAG follows, looking after him.

FAG: What! Thomas! Sure 'tis he? – What! Thomas! Thomas!

THOMAS: Hey! – Odd's life! Mr Fag! – give us your hand, my old fellow-servant.

FAG: Excuse my glove, Thomas: – I'm devilish glad to see you, my lad. Why, my prince of charioteers, you look as hearty! – but who the deuce thought of seeing you in Bath?

THOMAS: Sure, master, Madam Julia, Harry, Mrs Kate, and the postilion, be all come.

FAG: Indeed!

THOMAS: Ay, master thought another fit of the gout was coming to make him a visit; so he'd a mind to gi't the slip, and whip! we were all off at an hour's warning.

FAG: Ay, ay, hasty in everything, or it would not be Sir Anthony Absolute!

THOMAS: But tell us, Mr Fag, how does young master? Odd! Sir Anthony will stare to see the captain here!

FAG: I do not serve Captain Absolute now.

THOMAS: Why sure!

FAG: At present I am employed by Ensign Beverley.

THOMAS: I doubt, Mr Fag, you ha'n't changed for the better.

FAG: I have not changed, Thomas.

THOMAS: No! Why didn't you say you had left young master?

FAG: No. – Well, honest Thomas, I must puzzle you no farther: – briefly then – Captain Absolute and Ensign Beverley are one and the same person.

THOMAS: The devil they are!

FAG: So it is indeed, Thomas; and the ensign half of my master being on guard at present – the captain has nothing to do with me.

THOMAS: So, so! – What, this is some freak, I warrant! – Do tell us, Mr Fag, the meaning o't – you know I ha' trusted you.

FAG: You'll be secret, Thomas?

THOMAS: As a coach-horse.

FAG: Why then the cause of all this is – Love, – Love, Thomas, who (as you may get read to you) has been a masquerader ever since the days of Jupiter.

THOMAS: Ay, ay; – I guessed there was a lady in the case: – but pray, why does your master pass only for an ensign? – Now if he had shammed general indeed –

FAG: Ah! Thomas, there lies the mystery o'the matter.
Hark'ee, Thomas, my master is in love with a lady of
a very singular taste: a lady who likes him better as a
halfpay ensign than if she knew he was son and heir to
Sir Anthony Absolute, a baronet of three thousand a
year.

THOMAS: That is an odd taste indeed! – But has she got
the stuff, Mr Fag? Is she rich, hey?

FAG: Rich! – Why, I believe she owns half the stocks!
Zounds! Thomas, she could pay the national debt as
easily as I could my washerwoman! She has a lap-dog
that eats out of gold, – she feeds her parrot with small
pearls, – and all her thread-papers are made of
banknotes!

THOMAS: Bravo, faith! – Odd! I warrant she has a set
of thousands at least: – but does she draw kindly with
the captain?

FAG: As fond as pigeons.

THOMAS: May one hear her name?

FAG: Miss Lydia Languish. – But there is an old tough
aunt in the way; though, by-the-by, she has never seen
my master – for we got acquainted with miss while on
a visit in Gloucestershire.

THOMAS: Well – I wish they were once harnessed
together in matrimony. – But pray, Mr Fag, what kind
of a place is this Bath? – I ha' heard a deal of it –
here's a mort o'merry-making, hey?

FAG: Pretty well, Thomas, pretty well – 'tis a good
lounge; in the morning we go to the pump-room
(though neither my master nor I drink the waters);

after breakfast we saunter on the parades, or play a game at billiards; at night we dance; but damn the place, I'm tired of it: their regular hours stupefy me – not a fiddle nor a card after eleven! – However Mr Faulkland's gentleman and I keep it up a little in private parties; – I'll introduce you there, Thomas – you'll like him much.

THOMAS: Sure I know Mr Du-Peigne – you know his master is to marry Madam Julia.

FAG: I had forgot. – But, Thomas, you must polish a little – indeed you must. – Here now – this wig! What the devil do you do with a wig, Thomas? – None of the London whips of any degree of ton wear wigs now.

THOMAS: More's the pity! I more's the pity! I say – Odd's life! when I heard how the lawyers and doctors had took to their own hair, I thought how 'twould go next: – Odd rabbit it! when the fashion had got foot on the bar, I guessed 'twould mount to the box! – but 'tis all out of character, believe me, Mr Fag: and look'ee, I'll never gi' up mine – the lawyers and doctors may do as they will.

FAG: Well, Thomas, we'll not quarrel about that.

THOMAS: Why, bless you, the gentlemen of the professions ben't all of a mind – for in our village now, tho'ff Jack Gauge, the exciseman, has ta'en to his carrots, there's little Dick the farrier swears he'll never forsake his bob, though all the college should appear with their own heads!

FAG: Indeed! well said, Dick! – but hold – mark! mark! Thomas.

THOMAS: Zooks! 'tis the captain. – Is that the Lady

with him?

FAG: No, no, that is Madam Lucy, my master's mistress's maid. They lodge at that house – but I must after him to tell him the news.

THOMAS: Odd! he's given her money! – Well, Mr Fag –

FAG: Good-bye, Thomas. I have an appointment in Gyde's porch this evening at eight; meet me there, and we'll make a little party.

(*Exeunt severally.*)

THE IMPORTANCE OF BEING EARNEST (1895)

by Oscar Wilde

In Wilde's classic comedy of manners, JACK WORTHING and his friend ALGERNON MONCRIEFF are fashionable men about town. ALGERNON has discovered JACK's secret: JACK has invented a wicked younger brother named Ernest so that, using Ernest's behaviour as an excuse, he can escape from the country to London. ALGERNON also has an imaginary friend called Bunbury, to provide him with an excuse to escape London for the country. ALGERNON has turned up at JACK's country house and is pretending to be wicked Ernest. To complicate matters, JACK's ward, Cecily, has fallen in love with ALGERNON. JACK wishes to be engaged to ALGERNON's cousin, Gwendolen Fairfax, who is also visiting the house.

Act II

JACK: This ghastly state of things is what you call Bunburying, I suppose?

ALGERNON: Yes, and a perfectly wonderful Bunbury it is. The most wonderful Bunbury I have ever had in my life.

JACK: Well, you've no right whatsoever to Bunbury here.

ALGERNON: That is absurd. One has a right to Bunbury anywhere one chooses. Every serious Bunburyist knows that.

JACK: Serious Bunburyist! Good heavens!

ALGERNON: Well, one must be serious about something, if one wants to have any amusement in life. I happen to be serious about Bunburying. What on earth you are serious about I haven't got the remotest idea. About everything, I should fancy. You have such an absolutely trivial nature.

JACK: Well, the only small satisfaction I have in the whole of this wretched business is that your friend Bunbury is quite exploded. You won't be able to run down to the country quite so often as you used to do, dear Algy. And a very good thing too.

ALGERNON: Your brother is a little off colour, isn't he, dear Jack? You won't be able to disappear to London quite so frequently as your wicked custom was. And not a bad thing either.

JACK: As for your conduct towards Miss Cardew, I must say that your taking in a sweet, simple, innocent girl like that is quite inexcusable. To say nothing of the fact that she is my ward.

ALGERNON: I can see no possible defence at all for your deceiving a brilliant, clever, thoroughly experienced young lady like Miss Fairfax. To say nothing of the fact that she is my cousin.

JACK: I wanted to be engaged to Gwendolen, that is all. I love her.

ALGERNON: Well, I simply wanted to be engaged to Cecily. I adore her.

JACK: There is certainly no chance of your marrying Miss Cardew.

ALGERNON: I don't think there is much likelihood, Jack, of you and Miss Fairfax being united.

JACK: Well, that is no business of yours.

ALGERNON: If it was my business, I wouldn't talk about it. (*Begins to eat muffins.*) It is very vulgar to talk about one's business. Only people like stock-brokers do that, and then merely at dinner parties.

JACK: How you can sit there, calmly eating muffins when we are in this horrible trouble, I can't make out. You seem to me to be perfectly heartless.

ALGERNON: Well, I can't eat muffins in an agitated manner. The butter would probably get on my cuffs. One should always eat muffins quite calmly. It is the only way to eat them.

JACK: I say it's perfectly heartless your eating muffins at all, under the circumstances.

ALGERNON: When I am in trouble, eating is the only thing that consoles me. Indeed, when I am in really great trouble, as any one who knows me intimately will tell you, I refuse everything except food and drink. At the present moment I am eating muffins because I am unhappy. Besides, I am particularly fond of muffins. (*Rising.*)

JACK: (*Rising.*) Well, that is no reason why you should eat them all in that greedy way. (*Takes muffins from ALGERNON.*)

ALGERNON: (*Offering tea-cake.*) I wish you would have tea-cake instead. I don't like tea-cake.

JACK: Good heavens! I suppose a man may eat his own

muffins in his own garden.

ALGERNON: But you have just said it was perfectly heartless to eat muffins.

JACK: I said it was perfectly heartless of you, under the circumstances. That is a very different thing.

ALGERNON: That may be. But the muffins are the same. (*He seizes the muffin-dish from JACK.*)

JACK: Algy, I wish to goodness you would go.

ALGERNON: You can't possibly ask me to go without having some dinner. It's absurd. I never go without my dinner. No one ever does, except vegetarians and people like that. Besides I have just made arrangements with Dr Chasuble to be christened at a quarter to six under the name of Ernest.

JACK: My dear fellow, the sooner you give up that nonsense the better. I made arrangements this morning with Dr Chasuble to be christened myself at 5.30, and I naturally will take the name of Ernest. Gwendolen would wish it. We can't both be christened Ernest. It's absurd. Besides, I have a perfect right to be christened if I like. There is no evidence at all that I have ever been christened by anybody. I should think it extremely probable I never was, and so does Dr Chasuble. It is entirely different in your case. You have been christened already.

ALGERNON: Yes, but I have not been christened for years.

JACK: Yes, but you have been christened. That is the important thing.

ALGERNON: Quite so. So I know my constitution can

stand it. If you are not quite sure about your ever having been christened, I must say I think it rather dangerous your venturing on it now. It might make you very unwell. You can hardly have forgotten that some one very closely connected with you was very nearly carried off this week in Paris by a severe chill.

JACK: Yes, but you said yourself that a severe chill was not hereditary.

ALGERNON: It usen't to be, I know – but I daresay it is now. Science is always making wonderful improvements in things.

JACK: (*Picking up the muffin-dish.*) Oh, that is nonsense; you are always talking nonsense.

ALGERNON: Jack, you are at the muffins again! I wish you wouldn't. There are only two left. (*Takes them.*) I told you I was particularly fond of muffins.

JACK: But I hate tea-cake.

ALGERNON: Why on earth then do you allow tea-cake to be served up for your guests? What ideas you have of hospitality!

JACK: Algernon! I have already told you to go. I don't want you here. Why don't you go!

ALGERNON: I haven't quite finished my tea yet! and there is still one muffin left.

(*JACK groans, and sinks into a chair. ALGERNON still continues eating.*)

THE CHERRY ORCHARD (1906)

by Anton Chekhov
Version by Peter Gill

PUBLISHED BY OBERON BOOKS (ISBN 1 870 259 75 0)

The estate and cherry orchard belonging to the Gaev family have been auctioned off to pay their debts. The new owner is LOPAKHIN, a self-made man who was born as a serf on the land and now owns it. Formerly, he was the estate manager. On the day everyone is leaving, LOPAKHIN says his farewells to TROFIMOV, a perpetual student who has been a long-term hanger on of the family.

Act IV

LOPAKHIN: You wouldn't think it was October would you? It's still as fine as a summer day. Just the weather for building. (*He looks at his watch. Calls through the door.*) The train leaves in forty-seven minutes, ladies and gentlemen. Do you hear me? You ought to leave for the station in twenty minutes. You'd better hurry.

(*Enter TROFIMOV in a great coat.*)

TROFIMOV: It must be time to go. The horses are ready. Where the devil are my galoshes? Has anyone seen them? I've lost them. (*At the door.*) Anya! I can't find my galoshes!

LOPAKHIN: I'm spending the winter in Kharkov, so I'm travelling some of the way with you. I'll be glad to get to Kharkov, I can tell you. It's time I got back to work.

I've spent far too long sitting around here chattering to you all. I need to be working. I'm not cut out for sitting around talking. I don't know what to do with my hands if they're not working. They just seem to flap about.

TROFIMOV: Well you'll be rid of us soon and then you'll be able to take up your valuable labours without distraction.

LOPAKHIN: Would you like a glass of wine?

TROFIMOV: No thanks.

LOPAKHIN: You're going to Moscow I suppose.

TROFIMOV: Yes. I shall travel with them as far as town today, and then tomorrow I'll go on to Moscow.

LOPAKHIN: I dare say the Professors won't give any lectures until they know you've arrived safely.

TROFIMOV: What concern is it of yours?

LOPAKHIN: How many years is it that you've been at university?

TROFIMOV: Can't you think of anything better than that? That joke's worn a bit thin you know. (*Searches for galoshes.*) I suppose the likelihood is that we shall never see each other again. So here's a piece of advice at parting. Try and get out of the habit of waving your arms about. Will you? And another thing. Do you think these summer visitors of yours are really going to turn into farmers? Do you think your dream of an independent hardworking community is going to happen? That's not the way things are going to work out. I'm fond of you, you know. You have fine hands like an artist's. And you have a fine soul.

LOPAKHIN: (*Embraces him.*) Goodbye dear friend. Thank you. Are you alright for money? Are you sure? Let me give you some for the journey.

TROFIMOV: No thank you.

LOPAKHIN: But you haven't got a farthing.

TROFIMOV: Yes I have. I got some money for a translation. It's in here. Thanks all the same. (*Anxiously.*) I wish I knew where my galoshes were.

[VARYA: (*From another room.*) Here are the wretched things. (*She flings a pair of galoshes onto the stage.*)]

TROFIMOV: What's the matter, Varya? Eh? These aren't my galoshes.

LOPAKHIN: I sowed three thousand acres of poppies in the spring, and I've made at least forty thousand profit. You should have seen the poppy flowers when they were in bloom. What a sight. Wonderful. So you see I'm offering you a loan because I can afford it. I've just made forty thousand. Don't turn your nose up at me. Please. I don't mind talking about money. I'm a peasant, and I speak as I find.

TROFIMOV: Your father was a peasant and my father was a chemist. What does that mean? Absolutely nothing.

(*LOPAKHIN takes out his wallet.*)

No. I don't want any money. I really don't. Don't you realise that I wouldn't take two hundred thousand? I have to be free of all that. I don't want it. Everything that the rest of you want, the rich and the poor.

Possessions. Money. All that. It's no more to me than dust blown in the wind. I don't need you, you see. I've passed you by. And I'm proud of it. And strong because of it. Do you see? Humanity is on the march. It's moving towards the highest truth and happiness. And I'm in the front line.

LOPAKHIN: But will you get there?

TROFIMOV: Oh yes. I'll get there. (*Pause.*) I shall get there or show others the way.

(*In the distance, the sound of an axe striking a tree.*)

LOPAKHIN: It's time to go. Goodbye. Take care. We've no time for each other you and I. But life goes on without regard to our prejudices. Do you know, the only time I feel I exist is when I'm working – when I'm working so hard I've not time to think. I can see some point in it all then. But how many people are there in Russia who can say that? How many people in this country live to any purpose? Ah well. Never mind. I suppose that's what keeps the world turning.

II: MALE / FEMALE DUOLOGUES

ANTIGONE (442 BC)

by Sophocles
English version by Declan Donnellan

PUBLISHED BY OBERON BOOKS (ISBN 1 84002 136 5)

*The two sons of the banished King Oedipus have led a
failed rebellion against the tyrannical CREON, King of
Thebes. Both were killed, and CREON has given orders
that their bodies should remain unburied. In Greek
terms, this means that they cannot pass on to the
afterlife. However, their sister ANTIGONE has defied
the ban and scattered earth on their bodies. In this
scene, CREON confronts ANTIGONE.*

CREON: Please answer my questions very simply.
    Did you know I had decreed against this?

ANTIGONE: Of course I knew.

CREON: You dared to break the
                                            law?

ANTIGONE: Yes. It wasn't the law of Zeus I broke.
    Your decree laughs in the face of justice.
    It's perfectly simple: you have no right
    To pass such laws. You're just a little man,
    And you will die. How can you overturn
    The great enduring laws of the immortals?
    You can't rewrite them when you feel like it!
    For yesterday, tomorrow and today
    Dissolve within the greatness of their will.
    There's nothing brave in standing up to you.
    I'm far too scared to break my Gods' laws.
    Of course I knew that you'd put me to death:

It really didn't need a sham decree.
It doesn't matter so much when I die,
The sooner the better in fact. My pain
Is as wide as the sea; I want to die.
I do not want to see my mother's son
Stretched naked in the field and his white flesh
Pulled at by dogs. That I could not endure.
Do you think I'm a fool, Creon? Perhaps.
But then fools see fools everywhere, don't they?

[CHORUS: It's clear she gets her fierceness from her
                                                                        father.
He never taught her to yield to bad luck.]

CREON: The will that is too rigid often breaks,
Iron shatters if it cannot bend.
A tiny whip can tame the wildest horse.
Can you be a man and let yourself be cowed?
This woman knew exactly what she did.
The law was clear as glass, she shattered it
And stuck the fragments round her laughing head
To glitter like a crown. Let her go? No!
Then she would be the man, not me! Do I
Care that she's the daughter of my late sister?
It would be no different if she were
Every member of my family
Rolled into one. She and that sister of hers
Must suffer the full rigour of the law.
Oh yes, Ismene gave herself away –
Drag her here. I heard her in the palace,
Screeching, hysterical, out of control.
Guilt, gentlemen, will out. It drives me mad
To smell sin behind the mask of innocence.

ANTIGONE: Are you sure killing me will be enough?

CREON: That's all I want. Having this I have all.

ANTIGONE: Then why put it off? You go on and on:
    It hurts my ears; and what I say hurts you.
    What greater glory could I ever know
    Than when I lay my brother in the grave?
    These men here, they see me, they admire me,
    But don't worry, they won't say anything,
    They're scared of you. It must be nice to be
    A king – you can get away with murder.

CREON: You're on your own, it's only you who see
    Things like this.

ANTIGONE: On the contrary. These men
    See what I see but shut their mouths for you.

CREON: These are decent people. Aren't you ashamed
    To see things differently from them?

ANTIGONE: No,
    It is no shame to love your mother's child.

CREON: A pity Polynices didn't share
    Your view, Antigone: he died murdering
    The brother you conveniently forget.

ANTIGONE: His father and his mother both were mine.

CREON: Will Eteocles be pleased his sister
    Venerates his murderer?

ANTIGONE: Eteocles is dead. How can we know
    What he wants?

CREON: His ghost will rise and roar
    If you should praise his killer as his equal.

ANTIGONE: It wasn't his slave who died but his brother.

CREON: Your Polynices died invading Thebes.
  Eteocles was killed defending you.

ANTIGONE: Whatever you say all's one for the dead.
  The Gods want these rites.

CREON: So you think it's just
  The evil and the good receive the same?

ANTIGONE: These things are far too big for you to
                                        judge.

CREON: An enemy can never be a friend
  Even when he's dead.

ANTIGONE: I was not born to separate in hate.
  My mother gave me life to join in love.

CREON: I wonder who it is you really love?
  But hear this well. From now until I die
  No woman tells me how I ought to rule.

MEDEA (431 BC)

by Euripides
Translated by Alistair Elliot
PUBLISHED BY OBERON BOOKS (ISBN 1 870259 36 X)

MEDEA helped the hero Jason to defeat her father, the King of Colchis. He married her and she bore him two children. Returned to his home town of Thebes, Jason finds himself a national figure and is offered the hand in marriage of the King's daughter. To make this possible, he must divorce and abandon MEDEA, who will be banished from Thebes. MEDEA reacts violently to this news. Here, CREON the king comes to speak with her.

CREON: You sour-faced woman, squalling at your husband,
  Medea, I give you notice: you are banished.
  You must leave now. Now! Take your children with you.
  Don't make me wait. I shall not leave
  Until I've seen you off Corinthian land.

MEDEA: (*A cry.*)
  This is the end of everything, my last moment.
  My enemies speed me on with all sail set
  Towards the rocks – and there's no place to land.
  I have been much abused, but I still ask you,
  Creon, why are you sending me away?

CREON: I am afraid of you: no need to wrap
  The fact in phrases: I'm afraid that you
  Might do my daughter some irreparable harm.
  And many things contribute to this fear:
  You are clever; you have seen and known much evil;
  You are wounded, and deprived of bed and man.

And now I hear that you've been making threats
Against me, for giving my daughter to your husband.
I hear you will do something. I must guard against it.
Better to draw your hatred now than soften
And later have to weep for being soft.

MEDEA: (*Laughs bitterly.*)
Oh Creon, this is not the first time: often before
My reputation has done me harm, much harm.
My father, if he'd been wise, would never have had me
Taught to be clever, out of the ordinary.
That only makes you envied and disliked.
Try teaching new ideas to stupid people –
They think you're stupid, certainly not clever;
As for the others, who aspire to wit,
You offend them, too, if you are reckoned wittier.
I've had my share of that experience.
I am clever, so the jealous hate me – or
They find me difficult; but I'm not that clever.
Still, you're afraid of me. What do you think
I'll do to you to spoil your harmony?
You need not be on edge, Creon: look, I'm hardly
In a state for crimes against the crown.
What harm have *you* done *me*? It's my husband I hate,
Not you. You gave your daughter as your heart
                                        commanded.
That is your right, and seems to me quite sensible.
I don't resent things going well for you:
Celebrate marriage; prosper – all of you.
But let me stay. In spite of being wronged,
I'll keep the peace. You're stronger, and I've lost.

CREON: You seem to answer softly. But I shudder
To think what evil may be in your mind.
The softness makes me trust you even less.

For a hot-tempered woman – or man – is easier
To guard against than someone quiet and clever.
So you must leave. With no delay. No speeches.
The order's fixed. I know you are my enemy,
And you shall not contrive to stay among us.

MEDEA: I beg you, in the name of your newly-married
daughter.

CREON: Your words are wasted: you shall not persuade me.

MEDEA: You'll banish me? There's nothing I can say?

CREON: Why should I care for you more than my flesh
and blood?

MEDEA: My country! How much I think of home today!

CREON: It's what I care for most – except my children.

MEDEA: O Love, how great a curse you are to mortals!

CREON: Well, that depends upon the circumstance…

MEDEA: Zeus knows who caused all this: don't let him
get off free.

CREON: Move, woman. Must I have you dragged away?

MEDEA: No, Creon, no – not that. I'm pleading now…

CREON: So are you going to give me trouble? Yes or no?

MEDEA: We'll go, we'll leave – that isn't what I'm asking.

CREON: Why argue then? Why not just quietly go?

MEDEA: One day. Let me stay on for just one day.
Let me think out clearly where it is we'll go,
Make provision for the children, since their father
Puts rather low his duty to his sons.

Take pity on them: you're a father too;
It stands to reason you have kindness in you.
For my part, exile doesn't worry me –
I weep for them: they are so young to suffer.

CREON: I've never had the temper of a tyrant.
Often, from honouring other people's wishes,
I've spoiled things for myself – and even now
I see I might be making a mistake.
Still, you shall have your way. But in advance
I warn you, if the eye of heaven tomorrow
Should see you and your children on my soil,
You die. That is my word. As true as prophecy.
Remain then, if you must, this one day more:
Too short a time for you to do us harm.

(*Exit CREON.*)

HENRY VI PART 3 (c 1592)

by William Shakespeare

*The Wars of the Roses have torn England apart.
EDWARD IV has, through force of arms and the support
of a number of key noblemen, become King. EDWARD
is handsome, charming and libidinous. He needs a
Queen and an alliance with ELIZABETH GREY would
mean an alliance with the powerful Woodville family
and would greatly help to support his position. LADY
GREY is granted an audience in order to settle an
inheritance claim. EDWARD uses the opportunity to woo
her. LADY GREY is beautiful, intelligent and
manipulative. The scene is observed from a distance by
EDWARD's brothers, Clarence and Gloucester.*

Act III, Scene II

KING EDWARD IV: Now tell me, madam, do you love
your children?

LADY GREY: Ay, full as dearly as I love myself.

KING EDWARD IV: And would you not do much to do
them good?

LADY GREY: To do them good, I would sustain some harm.

KING EDWARD IV: Then get your husband's lands, to
do them good.

LADY GREY: Therefore I came unto your majesty.

KING EDWARD IV: I'll tell you how these lands are to
be got.

LADY GREY: So shall you bind me to your highness' service.

KING EDWARD IV: What service wilt thou do me, if I
                                  give them?

LADY GREY: What you command, that rests in me to do.

KING EDWARD IV: But you will take exceptions to my
                                  boon.

LADY GREY: No, gracious lord, except I cannot do it.

KING EDWARD IV: Ay, but thou canst do what I mean
                                  to ask.

LADY GREY: Why, then I will do what your grace
                                  commands.

[GLOUCESTER: (*Aside to Clarence.*)
    He plies her hard; and much rain wears the marble.

CLARENCE: (*Aside to Gloucester.*)
    As red as fire! nay, then her wax must melt.]

LADY GREY: Why stops my lord, shall I not hear my task?

KING EDWARD IV: An easy task; 'tis but to love a king.

LADY GREY: That's soon perform'd, because I am a subject.

KING EDWARD IV: Why, then, thy husband's lands I
                                  freely give thee.

LADY GREY: I take my leave with many thousand thanks.

[GLOUCESTER: (*Aside to Clarence.*)
    The match is made; she seals it with a curtsy.]

KING EDWARD IV: But stay thee, 'tis the fruits of love
                                  I mean.

LADY GREY: The fruits of love I mean, my loving liege.

KING EDWARD IV: Ay, but, I fear me, in another sense.
    What love, think'st thou, I sue so much to get?

LADY GREY: My love till death, my humble thanks, my
                                         prayers;
   That love which virtue begs and virtue grants.

KING EDWARD IV: No, by my troth, I did not mean
                                         such love.

LADY GREY: Why, then you mean not as I thought you did.

KING EDWARD IV: But now you partly may perceive my
                                         mind.

LADY GREY: My mind will never grant what I perceive
   Your highness aims at, if I aim aright.

KING EDWARD IV: To tell thee plain, I aim to lie with thee.

LADY GREY: To tell you plain, I had rather lie in prison.

KING EDWARD IV: Why, then thou shalt not have thy
                                         husband's lands.

LADY GREY: Why, then mine honesty shall be my dower;
   For by that loss I will not purchase them.

KING EDWARD IV: Therein thou wrong'st thy children
                                         mightily.

LADY GREY: Herein your highness wrongs both them
                                         and me.
   But, mighty lord, this merry inclination
   Accords not with the sadness of my suit:
   Please you dismiss me either with 'ay' or 'no'.

KING EDWARD IV: Ay, if thou wilt say 'ay' to my request;
   No if thou dost say 'no' to my demand.

LADY GREY: Then, no, my lord. My suit is at an end.

[GLOUCESTER: (*Aside to Clarence.*)
   The widow likes him not, she knits her brows.

CLARENCE: (*Aside to Gloucester.*)
He is the bluntest wooer in Christendom.]

KING EDWARD IV: (*Aside.*)
Her looks do argue her replete with modesty;
Her words do show her wit incomparable;
All her perfections challenge sovereignty:
One way or other, she is for a king;
And she shall be my love, or else my queen. –
Say that King Edward take thee for his queen?

LADY GREY: 'Tis better said than done, my gracious lord:
I am a subject fit to jest withal,
But far unfit to be a sovereign.

KING EDWARD VI: Sweet widow, by my state I swear
to thee
I speak no more than what my soul intends;
And that is, to enjoy thee for my love.

LADY GREY: And that is more than I will yield unto:
I know I am too mean to be your queen,
And yet too good to be your concubine.

KING EDWARD IV: You cavil, widow: I did mean, my
queen.

LADY GREY: 'Twill grieve your grace my sons should
call you father.

KING EDWARD IV: No more than when my daughters
call thee mother.
Thou art a widow, and thou hast some children;
And, by God's mother, I, being but a bachelor,
Have other some: why, 'tis a happy thing
To be the father unto many sons.
Answer no more, for thou shalt be my queen.

THE ROVER (1677)

by Aphra Behn

FLORINDA, a young woman of quality, is escaping from her house in the middle of the night, to meet with her lover, BELVILE. Unfortunately, as she escapes her governess, Callis, and reaches the garden, whom should she find there but WILLMORE, a penniless but dashing Sea Captain newly landed in Naples. WILLMORE is very drunk and FLORINDA immediately recognises that both her reputation and her person are in danger.

Act III, Scene III

Enter FLORINDA undress'd, with a Key, and a little Box.

FLORINDA: Well, thus far I'm in my way to happiness; I have got my self free from Callis; my brother too, I find by yonder light, is gone into his cabinet,[1] and thinks not of me: I have by good fortune got the key of the garden back-door, – I'll open it, to prevent Belvile's knocking, – a little noise will now alarm my brother. Now am I as fearful as a young Thief.

(*Unlocks the door.*)

– Hark – what noise is that? – Oh 'twas the wind that played amongst the boughs. – Belvile stays long, methinks – it's time – stay for fear of a surprise, I'll hide these jewels in yonder jessamine.[2]

(*She goes to lay down the Box. Enter WILLMORE drunk.*)

---

1   *cabinet* Chamber
2   *jessamine* Shrub

WILLMORE: What the Devil is become of these fellows, Belvile and Frederick? They promis'd to stay at the next corner for me, but who the Devil knows the corner of a full moon? – Now – whereabouts am I? – hah – what have we here? a garden! – a very convenient place to sleep in – hah – what has God sent us here? – a female – by this light, a woman; I'm a dog if it be not a very wench. –

FLORINDA: He's come! – hah – who's there?

WILLMORE: Sweet soul, let me salute thy shoe-string.

FLORINDA: 'Tis not my Belvile – good Heavens, I know him not. – Who are you, and from whence come you?

WILLMORE: Prithee – prithee; child – not so many hard questions – let it suffice I am here, child – Come, come kiss me.

FLORINDA: Good Gods! What luck is mine!

WILLMORE: Only good luck, child, parlous good luck. – Come hither, – 'tis a delicate shining wench, – by this hand she's perfum'd, and smells like any nosegay. – Prithee, dear soul, let's not play the fool, and lose time, – precious time – for as God shall save me, I'm as honest a fellow as breathes, tho I am a little disguis'd at present. – Come, I say, – why, thou may'st be free with me, I'll be very secret. I'll not boast who 'twas oblig'd me, not I – for hang me if I know thy name.

FLORINDA: Heavens! what a filthy beast is this!

WILLMORE: I am so, and thou oughtst the sooner to lie with me for that reason, – for look you, child, there will be no sin in't, because 'twas neither design'd nor

premeditated; 'tis pure accident on both sides – that's
a certain thing now – Indeed should I make love to
you, and you vow fidelity – and swear and lie till you
believ'd and yielded – Thou art therefore (as thou art
a good Christian) oblig'd in conscience to deny me
nothing. Now – come, be kind, without any more idle
prating.

FLORINDA: Oh, I am ruin'd – wicked man, unhand me.

WILLMORE: Wicked! Egad, child, a judge, were he
young and vigorous, and saw those eyes of thine,
would know 'twas they gave the first blow – the first
provocation. – Come, prithee let's lose no time, I say –
this is a fine convenient place.

FLORINDA: Sir, let me go, I conjure you, or I'll call out.

WILLMORE: Ay, ay, you were best to call witness to see
how finely you treat me – do –

FLORINDA: I'll cry murder, rape, or any thing, if you do
not instantly let me go.

WILLMORE: A rape! Come, come, you lie, you baggage,
you lie: What, I'll warrant you would fain have the
world believe now that you are not so forward as I.
No, not you, – why at this time of night was your
cobweb-door set open, dear spider – but to catch
flies? – Hah come – or I shall be damnably angry. –
Why what a coil is here. –

FLORINDA: Sir, can you think –

WILLMORE: That you'd do it for nothing? oh, oh, I find
what you'd be at – look here, here's a pistole[3] for you
– here's a work indeed – here – take it, I say. –

3 *pistole* Coin

FLORINDA: For Heaven's sake, sir, as you're a
    gentleman –

WILLMORE: So – now – she would be wheedling me
    for more – what, you will not take it then – you're
    resolv'd you will not. – Come, come, take it, or I'll put
    it up again; for, look ye, I never give more. – Why,
    how now, mistress, are you so high i'th' mouth, a
    pistole won't down with you? – hah – why, what a
    work's here – in good time – come, no struggling, be
    gone – But an y'are good at a dumb wrestle, I'm for
    ye, – look ye, – I'm for ye. –

(She struggles with him.)

THE PLAIN DEALER (1676)

by William Wycherley

This comedy concerns the cynical and misanthropic MANLY, a bluntly-spoken sea captain and adventurer. He has recently returned from the Dutch wars. Having left his fortune with his beloved Olivia, he now finds he is betrayed – Olivia has stolen the money and married his best friend. FIDELIA is a young woman in love with MANLY, who has disguised herself as a boy and followed him to sea, becoming his loyal friend. Here, having just discovered Olivia's cruel trick, MANLY persuades FIDELIA (still unrecognised and in men's clothes) to get his revenge for him.

Act III, Scene I

FIDELIA: Sir, good Sir, generous Captain.

MANLY: Pr'ythee, kind Impertinence, leave me. Why shou'dst thou follow me, flatter my Generosity now, since thou know'st I have no Money left? if I had it, I'd give it thee, to buy my quiet.

FIDELIA: I never follow'd yet, Sir, Reward or Fame, but you alone; nor do I now beg any thing, but leave to share your miseries: You shou'd not be a Niggard of 'em, since, methinks, you have enough to spare. Let me follow you now, because you hate me, as you have often said.

MANLY: I ever hated a Coward's company, I must confess.

FIDELIA: Let me follow you, till I am none then; for you, I'm sure, will through such Worlds of dangers, that I shall be inur'd to 'em; nay, I shall be afraid of your anger more than danger, and so turn valiant out of fear. Dear Captain, do not cast me off, till you have try'd me once more: do not, do not go to Sea again without me.

MANLY: Thou to Sea! to Court, thou Fool; remember the advice I gave thee: thou art a handsom Spaniel, and canst faun naturally; go, busk about,[1] and run thy self into the next great Man's Lobby: first faun upon the Slaves without, and then run into the Ladies Bed-chamber; thou may'st be admitted, at last, to tumble her Bed: go, seek, I say, and lose me; for I am not able to keep thee: I have not Bread for my self.

FIDELIA: Therefore I will not go, because then I may help and serve you.

MANLY: Thou!

FIDELIA: I warrant you, Sir; for, at worst, I cou'd beg or steal for you.

MANLY: Nay, more bragging! dost thou not know there's venturing your life, in stealing? Go, pr'ythee, away: thou art as hard to shake off, as that flattering effeminating mischief, Love.

FIDELIA: Love, did you name? Why, you are not so miserable as to be yet in Love, sure!

MANLY: No, no, pr'ythee away, be gone, or – (*Aside.*) I had almost discover'd my Love and Shame; well, if I had? that thing cou'd not think the worse of me: – or if he did? – no – yes, he shall know it – he shall – but then I must never leave him, for they are such secrets, that make Parasites and Pimps Lords of their Masters;

---

1   *busk about*   Of a ship – to beat or cruise about

for any slavery or tyranny is easier than Love's. (*To FIDELIA once more.*) Come hither. Since thou art so forward to serve me, hast thou but resolution enough to endure the torture of a secret? for such, to some, is unsupportable.

FIDELIA: I wou'd keep it as safe, as if your dear precious life depended on't.

MANLY: Dam your dearness. It concerns more than my life, my honour.

FIDELIA: Doubt it not, Sir.

MANLY: And do not discover it, by too much fear of discovering it; but have a great care you let not *Freeman* find it out.

FIDELIA: I warrant you, Sir. I am already all joy, with the hopes of your commands; and shall be all wings, in the execution of 'em: speak quickly, Sir.

MANLY: You said you wou'd beg for me.

FIDELIA: I did, Sir.

MANLY: Then you shall beg for me.

FIDELIA: With all my heart, Sir.

MANLY: That is, Pimp for me.

FIDELIA: How, Sir?

MANLY: D'ye start! thinkst thou, thou cou'dst do me any other service? Come, no dissembling honour: I know you can do it handsomly, thou wert made for't: You have lost your time with me at Sea, you must recover it.

FIDELIA: Do not, Sir, beget your self more Reasons for your Aversion to me, and make my obedience to you a fault: I am the unfittest in the World, to do you such a service.

MANLY: Your cunning arguing against it, shews but how fit you are for it. No more dissembling: here, (I say) you must go use it for me, to *Olivia*.

FIDELIA: To her, Sir?

MANLY: Go flatter, lie, kneel, promise, any thing to get her for me: I cannot live, unless I have her. Didst thou not say thou wou'dst do any thing, to save my life? And she said you had a persuading face.

FIDELIA: But, did not you say, Sir, your honour was dearer to you, than your life? And wou'd you have me contribute to the loss of that, and carry love from you, to the most infamous, most false, and –

MANLY: And most beautiful! – (*Sighs aside.*)

FIDELIA: Most ungrateful Woman, that ever liv'd; for sure she must be so, that cou'd desert you so soon, use you so basely, and so lately too: do not, do not forget it, Sir, and think –

MANLY: No, I will not forget it, but think of revenge: I will lie with her, out of revenge. Go, be gone, and prevail for me, or never see me more.

FIDELIA: You scorn'd her last night.

MANLY: I know not what I did last night; I dissembled last night.

FIDELIA: Heavens!

MANLY: Be gone, I say, and bring me love or compliance back, or hopes at least, or I'll never see thy face again: by –

FIDELIA: O do not swear, Sir, first hear me.

MANLY: I am impatient, away, you'll find me here till twelve. (*Turns away.*)

FIDELIA: Sir –

MANLY: Not one word, no insinuating Argument more, or soothing persuasion; you'll have need of all your Rhetorick with her: go, strive to alter her, not me; be gone.

DON JUAN (1736)

by Carlo Goldoni
Translated by Robert David MacDonald

PUBLISHED BY OBERON BOOKS (ISBN 1 870259 37 8)

The play is set in eighteenth-century Spain. Don Juan is the legendary seducer and corrupter of women. He has just seduced a shepherdess, ELISA, and unfortunately her betrothed, CARINO, has seen her disappear up the mountain with Don Juan. Here, CARINO confronts ELISA and she has to use all her verbal skills to defuse the situation.

Act II

CARINO: Are you back so late?

ELISA: Listen, Carino.
   My pet, white deer I love so much, I heard it –
   crying: I ran to it in fear… Quite often
   I wondered whether I would arrive in time.

CARINO: Be honest: may it not have been a stag,
   that by its barking tempted you away?

ELISA: We don't get stags here.

CARINO: Only I thought I saw
   you with an animal which was no deer.

ELISA: You are mistaken.

CARINO: No, there was no mistake;
   it was an animal like us.

ELISA: You mean
   a man?

CARINO: I do.

ELISA: Oh, him! that was a cousin
of Corydon's, the one goes with Nerina;
he's just a stupid shepherd, but the others
find him amusing with the things he says.

CARINO: I see: and you find him still more amusing.

ELISA: He certainly makes me laugh.

CARINO: One day – who knows? –
he may also make you cry?

ELISA: Why ever should he?

CARINO: Enough…what is his name?

ELISA: What are you asking?
You mean you didn't recognise Pagoro?

CARINO: I never saw him look so spruce, so proud!

ELISA: (I fear things are beginning to come out.)

CARINO: What did he promise, and swear to do for you?

ELISA: To find a companion for my little deer.

CARINO: (The little deer has certainly found that.)
It seemed I heard the name of wife.

ELISA: Well, that
would make my deer a wife.

CARINO: From what I heard
it seemed the wife was going to be you.

ELISA: The stupid fellow said, if all the beauties
in the world proposed themselves to him in marriage,
he wouldn't be the leastest bit surprised.

CARINO: Has he gone on to the city?

ELISA: Yes, to sell
    Nerina's flowers for her.

CARINO: And taken with him
    Elisa's heart.

ELISA: What was that?

CARINO: Oh, be quiet!
    I know it all, I heard it all. You liar,
    you cannot hide things from me now.

ELISA: Carino!
    How can you talk to me that way?

CARINO: That is
    the way Carino talks to perjurers,
    who have betrayed him. Do you not remember
    the faith you swore to me? Ungrateful! Cruel!
    Could you not keep faith a single day?

ELISA: Listen to me…you must not think…

CARINO: Be quiet!
    I do not want to hear another word.
    You want to weave another web of lies
    and flattery around my heart. If ever
    I lend an ear again to such deceptions,
    then I deserve to be betrayed, and worse.

ELISA: (I cannot hide my fault a second longer.)
    Carino, oh, my life! It is all too true:
    the man you saw me with wished to deceive me.
    I had been drawn to him at first by pity:
    attacked by robbers, he'd called out for help,
    and to reward me for the aid I gave him
    he offered me his hand and, flattering me
    with all the crafty townsman's thousand arts

and wiles, brought me to feel some silly sort
of infatuation for him. But, Carino,
I still remembered you, and kept my heart
constant and faithful.

CARINO: I am miserable!
If only I had never heard your words.
I leave you; I abandon you; I curse
the day I met you.

ELISA: No, you must not leave me!
I am so wretched! do you not remember
those days we spent together…

CARINO: Yes, I do,
and to my greater pain. Much as I loved you,
I swear I hate you now.

ELISA: Look, at your feet
your poor Elisa asks forgiveness for
her innocent mistake. Have pity, dearest.

CARINO: Do not hope for it – ever.

ELISA: If you are
my life, ah, then I cannot live without you.

CARINO: Your life is of no interest to me.

ELISA: In that case, I must die here at your feet.

CARINO: And I shall watch you do so with great
    pleasure.

ELISA: (I knew how he would hate me.) With this blade –
look at me! – I'll kill myself!

CARINO: (*Not looking.*)   Go on, then.
Pierce your unworthy heart, and wash away
the stain you have put upon my love and faith.

ELISA: I am not afraid of dying. The only thing
that *can* make me afraid is your contempt;
oh, do not let me die without a glance.
Look at me once more in charity,
then I shall kill myself.

CARINO: You need not hope
for that from me.

ELISA: Oh, God! You are inhuman!
Would you deny me even that small comfort?
Do my tears not move you to an ounce of pity?
It is so little, the favour that I ask;
look at me once, and then I shall be gone.

CARINO: (She is melting me.) You miserable creature,
there, I shall look at you. What is it you want?
(The sight is fatal.) You do not move my pity.
(I cannot resist it.)

ELISA: (He is beginning to yield.)
Oh, God, I can control myself no longer:
the terrible bitter pain has done the office
better than any sword: I fall, I die.

(*She pretends to faint.*)

CARINO: Elisa! Heavens! What is this? Are you dead?
No, she's not dead. Run to the nearby spring,
fetch water and run back; cases of fainting
can be brought round with water in the face.

(*He goes out.*)

ELISA: The ninny has surrendered! Oh, the joy
of knowing how to pretend at the right time.

THE BATTLEFIELD (1760)

by Carlo Goldoni
Translated by Robert David MacDonald
PUBLISHED BY OBERON BOOKS (ISBN 1 870259 37 8)

A city is under siege. The CONTE, a lieutenant in the defending army, always has an eye out for the main chance. So when LISETTA, a country girl with food to sell so that she can support her family, arrives in the city, he is quick to make his move. It is not only the contents of LISETTA's basket that he is interested in.

Act I

LISETTA: My eggs, my cheese, bring it back! What will my mother say? *Povera me.* (*In tears.*)

CONTE: (*Enters with CORPORAL.*) Child, child, what is the matter?

LISETTA: They stole my eggs and my cheese.

CONTE: What villains were these?

LISETTA: Two soldiers.

CONTE: Where did they go?

LISETTA: Them there, them two jumping about. Pretended to fight, and then ran off, and now they're laughing for having cheated me. Big joke for them. My mother will kill me, so she will.

CONTE: Corporal, go and arrest these two. The General gave order not a pin was to be looted during the truce, on pain of death. Take them straight to the provost-marshal and have them hanged as they deserve. And you can hang that mirror opposite them. Give them something to watch.

(*CORPORAL leaves.*)

LISETTA: That's not going to get my eggs and cheese back.

CONTE: Hush, hush now. How much was it all worth?

LISETTA: Four paoli.

CONTE: All this crying for four paoli?

LISETTA: My mother will kill me, so she will.

CONTE: Come now, if it'll stop you crying, here are your four paoli.

LISETTA: Is that really four paoli?

CONTE: Do you think I'm trying to cheat you?

LISETTA: I don't trust nobody.

CONTE: I am an officer and a gentleman.

LISETTA: I'll still count them all the same.

CONTE: Well, is it all there?

LISETTA: Don't I get nothing for the fright I had?

CONTE: That is an entirely different matter. Have you nothing left to sell?

LISETTA: Fruit.

CONTE: How much?

LISETTA: Three paoli.

CONTE: Here's a zecchino.

LISETTA: I can't change your money, signore.

CONTE: Then bring it to my quarters.

LISETTA: (*In exaggerated refusal.*) *Marameo*!

CONTE: And what is that supposed to mean?

LISETTA: I'm not going to no officer's quarters.

CONTE: Your exquisite reason, child?

LISETTA: Not after what happened…to my mother.

CONTE: And what exactly did happen to your mother?

LISETTA: I don't know, but I'm not going.

CONTE: Keep your fruit then.

LISETTA: And the three paoli?

CONTE: Nothing is for nothing in this world, girl.

LISETTA: (*Crying.*) Oh, that's nice, so it is. You promise me three paoli, and now you won't give me nothing.

CONTE: (She's playing the innocent, but I think she's cunning as the devil.)

LISETTA: You said you'd give me three paoli for the fruit, what I was going to sell. Here it is then, if you don't want to pay me, who cares? (*Throws the fruit on the ground, in tears the while.*)

CONTE: I'm not refusing you three paoli, or six, or ten or whatever you want, I just want you to be nice to me.

LISETTA: I am nice.

CONTE: That's better. What's your name?

LISETTA: Lisetta.

CONTE: Is your mother alive, Lisetta?

LISETTA: Yes, and she'll kill me when…

CONTE: And your father?

LISETTA: Ehi, *poverino*. He's dead, and it's because of your war. He wore himself out chopping wood for your officers, and he just dropped dead, so you'd better give me something for my father. Who's dead.

CONTE: Come, come, whatever you want: just stop crying.

LISETTA: What'll you give me if I do?

CONTE: A scudo?

LISETTA: And if I laugh?

CONTE: A zecchino?

LISETTA: (*Laughing.*) Come on then.

CONTE: Come to my quarters.

LISETTA: Here, you can't believe none of you. Liars one and all.

CONTE: Lisetta.

LISETTA: Leave me be.

CONTE: Look at this pretty zecchino.

LISETTA: (*Laughing.*) For me?

CONTE: For you.

LISETTA: (*Laughing.*) You giving it to me?

CONTE: If you come to my quarters.

LISETTA: Rot your quarters.

SHE STOOPS TO CONQUER (1773)

by Oliver Goldsmith

MARLOW's father wants him to marry the daughter of a country gentleman, Hardcastle. MARLOW has an unfortunate affliction – though he has no problem at all flirting with women of the lower classes, he finds himself tongue-tied and embarrassed with women of his own rank. By a set of unexpected circumstances and deliberate deceptions, MARLOW finds himself staying at Hardcastle's house but believes it to be a country inn. He therefore believes that KATE HARDCASTLE is a barmaid, and just the kind of woman whose company he enjoys. KATE has worked out what is going on and happily plays along.

Act III

MARLOW: What a bawling in every part of the house! I have scarce a moment's repose. If I go to the best room, there I find my host and his story: if I fly to the gallery, there we have my hostess with her curtsy down to the ground. I have at last got a moment to myself, and now for recollection. (*Walks and muses.*)

MISS HARDCASTLE: Did you call, sir? Did your honour call?

MARLOW: (*Musing.*) As for Miss Hardcastle, she's too grave and sentimental for me.

MISS HARDCASTLE: Did your honour call?

(*She still places herself before him, he turning away.*)

MARLOW: No, child. (*Musing.*) Besides, from the glimpse I had of her, I think she squints.

MISS HARDCASTLE: I'm sure, sir, I heard the bell ring.

MARLOW: No, no. (*Musing.*) I have pleased my father, however, by coming down, and I'll to-morrow please myself by returning.

(*Taking out his tablets, and perusing.*)

MISS HARDCASTLE: Perhaps the other gentleman called, sir?

MARLOW: I tell you, no.

MISS HARDCASTLE: I should be glad to know, sir. We have such a parcel of servants!

MARLOW: No, no, I tell you. (*Looks full in her face.*) Yes, child, I think I did call. I wanted – I wanted – I vow, child, you are vastly handsome.

MISS HARDCASTLE: O la, sir, you'll make one ashamed.

MARLOW: Never saw a more sprightly malicious eye. Yes, yes, my dear, I did call. Have you got any of your – a – what d'ye call it in the house?

MISS HARDCASTLE: No, sir, we have been out of that these ten days.

MARLOW: One may call in this house, I find, to very little purpose. Suppose I should call for a taste, just by way of a trial, of the nectar of your lips; perhaps I might be disappointed in that too.

MISS HARDCASTLE: Nectar! nectar! That's a liquor there's no call for in these parts. French, I suppose. We sell no French wines here, sir.

MARLOW: Of true English growth, I assure you.

MISS HARDCASTLE: Then it's odd I should not know it. We brew all sorts of wines in this house, and I have lived here these eighteen years.

MARLOW: Eighteen years! Why, one would think, child, you kept the bar before you were born. How old are you?

MISS HARDCASTLE: O! sir, I must not tell my age. They say women and music should never be dated.

MARLOW: To guess at this distance, you can't be much above forty (*Approaching.*) Yet, nearer, I don't think so much (*Approaching.*) By coming close to some women they look younger still; but when we come very close indeed – (*Attempting to kiss her.*)

MISS HARDCASLTE: Pray, sir, keep your distance. One would think you wanted to know one's age, as they do horses, by mark of mouth.

MARLOW: I protest, child, you use me extremely ill. If you keep me at this distance, how is it possible you and I can ever be acquainted?

MISS HARDCASTLE: And who wants to be acquainted with you? I want no such acquaintance, not I. I'm sure you did not treat Miss Hardcastle, that was here awhile ago, in this obstropalous manner. I'll warrant me, before her you looked dashed, and kept bowing to the ground, and talked, for all the world, as if you was before a justice of peace.

MARLOW: (*Aside.*) Egad, she has hit it, sure enough! (*To her.*) In awe of her, child? Ha! ha! ha! A mere awkward squinting thing; no, no. I find you don't know

me. I laughed and rallied her a little; but I was
unwilling to be too severe. No, I could not be too
severe, curse me!

MISS HARDCASTLE: O! then, sir, you are a favourite, I
find, among the ladies?

MARLOW: Yes, my dear, a great favourite. And yet
hang me, I don't see what they find in me to follow. At
the Ladies' Club in town I'm called their agreeable
Rattle. Rattle, child, is not my real name, but one I'm
known by. My name is Solomons; Mr Solomons, my
dear, at your service.

(*Offering to salute her.*)

MISS HARDCASTLE: Hold, sir; you are introducing me
to your club, not to yourself. And you're so great a
favourite there, you say?

MARLOW: Yes, my dear. There's Mrs Mantrap, Lady
Betty Blackleg, the Countess of Sligo, Mrs Langhorns,
old Miss Biddy Buckskin, and your humble servant,
keep up the spirit of the place.

MISS HARDCASTLE: Then it's a very merry place, I
suppose?

MARLOW: Yes, as merry as cards, supper, wine, and old
women can make us.

MISS HARDCASTLE: And their agreeable Rattle, ha!
ha! ha!

MARLOW: (*Aside.*) Egad! I don't quite like this chit. She
looks knowing, methinks. You laugh, child?

MISS HARDCASTLE: I can't but laugh, to think what
time they all have for minding their work or their
family.

MARLOW: (*Aside.*) All's well; she don't laugh at me. (*To her.*) Do you ever work, child?

MISS HARDCASTLE: Ay, sure. There's not a screen or quilt in the whole house but what can bear witness to that.

MARLOW: Odso! then you must show me your embroidery. I embroider and draw patterns myself a little. If you want a judge of your work, you must apply to me. (*Seizing her hand.*)

MISS HARDCASTLE: Ay, but the colours do not look well by candlelight. You shall see all in the morning. (*Struggling.*)

MARLOW: And why not now, my angel? Such beauty fires beyond the power of resistance. – Pshaw! the father here! My old luck: I never nicked seven that I did not throw an ace three times following.

(*Exit MARLOW as HARDCASTLE enters.*)

AN IDEAL HUSBAND (1895)

by Oscar Wilde

Witty, spirited MABEL CHILTERN has made a successful debut in high society, and has always known that she and dapper, ironic LORD GORING are an ideal match for one another. It has taken LORD GORING a little longer to see this but now the scales have dropped from his eyes and it is time for them both to acknowledge where their future happiness lies.

Act IV

MABEL CHILTERN: (*Takes up roses and begins to arrange them in a bowl on the table.*) People who don't keep their appointments in the Park are horrid.

LORD GORING: Detestable.

MABEL CHILTERN: I am glad you admit it. But I wish you wouldn't look so pleased about it.

LORD GORING: I can't help it. I always look pleased when I am with you.

MABEL CHILTERN: (*Sadly.*) Then I suppose it is my duty to remain with you?

LORD GORING: Of course it is.

MABEL CHILTERN: Well, my duty is a thing I never do, on principle. It always depresses me. So I am afraid I must leave you.

LORD GORING: Please don't, Miss Mabel. I have something very particular to say to you.

MABEL CHILTERN: (*Rapturously.*) Oh! is it a proposal?

LORD GORING: (*Somewhat taken aback.*) Well, yes, it is – I am bound to say it is.

MABEL CHILTERN: (*With a sigh of pleasure.*) I am so glad. That makes the second to-day.

LORD GORING: (*Indignantly.*) The second to-day? What conceited ass has been impertinent enough to dare to propose to you before I had proposed to you?

MABEL CHILTERN: Tommy Trafford, of course. It is one of Tommy's days for proposing. He always proposes on Tuesdays and Thursdays, during the Season.

LORD GORING: You didn't accept him, I hope?

MABEL CHILTERN: I make it a rule never to accept Tommy. That is why he goes on proposing. Of course, as you didn't turn up this morning, I very nearly said yes. It would have been an excellent lesson both for him and for you if I had. It would have taught you both better manners.

LORD GORING: Oh! bother Tommy Trafford. Tommy is a silly little ass. I love you.

MABEL CHILTERN: I know. And I think you might have mentioned it before. I am sure I have given you heaps of opportunities.

LORD GORING: Mabel, do be serious. Please be serious.

MABEL CHILTERN: Ah! that is the sort of thing a man always says to a girl before he has been married to her. He never says it afterwards.

LORD GORING: (*Taking hold of her hand.*) Mabel, I

have told you that I love you. Can't you love me a little in return?

MABEL CHILTERN: You silly Arthur! If you knew anything about…anything, which you don't, you would know that I adore you. Every one in London knows it except you. It is a public scandal the way I adore you. I have been going about for the last six months telling the whole of society that I adore you. I wonder you consent to have anything to say to me. I have no character left at all. At least, I feel so happy that I am quite sure I have no character left at all.

LORD GORING: (*Catches her in his arms and kisses her. Then there is a pause of bliss.*) Dear! Do you know I was awfully afraid of being refused!

MABEL CHILTERN: (*Looking up at him.*) But you never have been refused yet by anybody, have you, Arthur? I can't imagine anyone refusing you.

LORD GORING: (*After kissing her again.*) Of course I'm not nearly good enough for you, Mabel.

MABEL CHILTERN: (*Nestling close to him.*) I am so glad, darling. I was afraid you were.

LORD GORING: (*After some hesitation.*) And I'm… I'm a little over thirty.

MABEL CHILTERN: Dear, you look weeks younger than that.

LORD GORING: (*Enthusiastically.*) How sweet of you to say so! …And it is only fair to tell you frankly that I am fearfully extravagant.

MABEL CHILTERN: But so am I, Arthur. So we're sure

to agree. And now I must go and see Gertrude.

LORD GORING: Must you really? (*Kisses her.*)

MABEL CHILTERN: Yes.

LORD GORING: Then do tell her I want to talk to her particularly. I have been waiting here all the morning to see either her or Robert.

MABEL CHILTERN: Do you mean to say you didn't come here expressly to propose to me?

LORD GORING: (*Triumphantly.*) No; that was a flash of genius.

MABEL CHILTERN: Your first.

LORD GORING: (*With determination.*) My last.

MABEL CHILTERN: I am delighted to hear it. Now don't stir. I'll be back in five minutes. And don't fall into any temptations while I am away.

LORD GORING: Dear Mabel, while you are away, there are none. It makes me horribly dependent on you.

THE IMPORTANCE OF BEING EARNEST (1895)

by Oscar Wilde

JACK WORTHING, a wealthy young man in fashionable society, has fallen for the charms of the wealthy heiress GWENDOLEN FAIRFAX. At the rooms of her cousin Algy, JACK proposes to GWENDOLEN. She does not know his secret, believing his first name to be 'Ernest', not Jack.

Act I

JACK: Charming day it has been, Miss Fairfax.

GWENDOLEN: Pray don't talk to me about the weather, Mr Worthing. Whenever people talk to me about the weather, I always feel quite certain that they mean something else. And that makes me so nervous.

JACK: I do mean something else.

GWENDOLEN: I thought so. In fact, I am never wrong.

JACK: And I would like to be allowed to take advantage of Lady Bracknell's temporary absence...

GWENDOLEN: I would certainly advise you to do so. Mamma has a way of coming back suddenly into a room that I have often had to speak to her about.

JACK: (*Nervously.*) Miss Fairfax, ever since I met you I have admired you more than any girl...I have ever met since...I met you.

GWENDOLEN: Yes, I am quite well aware of the fact.

And I often wish that in public, at any rate, you had been more demonstrative. For me you have always had an irresistible fascination. Even before I met you I was far from indifferent to you.

(*JACK looks at her in amazement.*)

We live, as I hope you know, Mr Worthing, in an age of ideals. The fact is constantly mentioned in the more expensive monthly magazines, and has reached the provincial pulpits, I am told; and my ideal has always been to love some one of the name of Ernest. There is something in that name that inspires absolute confidence. The moment Algernon first mentioned to me that he had a friend called Ernest, I knew I was destined to love you.

JACK: You really love me, Gwendolen?

GWENDOLEN: Passionately!

JACK: Darling! You don't know how happy you've made me.

GWENDOLEN: My own Ernest!

JACK: But you don't really mean to say that you couldn't love me if my name wasn't Ernest?

GWENDOLEN: But your name is Ernest.

JACK: Yes, I know it is. But supposing it was something else? Do you mean to say you couldn't love me then?

GWENDOLEN: (*Glibly*) Ah! that is clearly a metaphysical speculation, and like most metaphysical speculations has very little reference at all to the actual facts of real life, as we know them.

JACK: Personally, darling, to speak quite candidly, I don't much care about the name of Ernest... I don't think the name suits me at all.

GWENDOLEN: It suits you perfectly. It is a divine name. It has a music of its own. It produces vibrations.

JACK: Well, really, Gwendolen, I must say that I think there are lots of other much nicer names. I think Jack, for instance, a charming name.

GWENDOLEN: Jack?... No, there is very little music in the name Jack, if any at all, indeed. It does not thrill. It produces absolutely no vibrations... I have known several Jacks, and they all, without exception, were more than usually plain. Besides, Jack is a notorious domesticity for John! And I pity any woman who is married to a man called John. She would probably never be allowed to know the entrancing pleasure of a single moment's solitude. The only really safe name is Ernest.

JACK: Gwendolen, I must get christened at once – I mean we must get married at once. There is no time to be lost.

GWENDOLEN: Married, Mr Worthing?

JACK: (*Astounded.*) Well...surely. You know that I love you, and you led me to believe, Miss Fairfax, that you were not absolutely indifferent to me.

GWENDOLEN: I adore you. But you haven't proposed to me yet. Nothing has been said at all about marriage. The subject has not even been touched on.

JACK: Well...may I propose to you now?

GWENDOLEN: I think it would be an admirable opportunity. And to spare you any possible disappointment, Mr Worthing, I think it only fair to tell you quite frankly before-hand that I am fully determined to accept you.

JACK: Gwendolen!

GWENDOLEN: Yes, Mr Worthing, what have you got to say to me?

JACK: You know what I have got to say to you.

GWENDOLEN: Yes, but you don't say it.

JACK: Gwendolen, will you marry me? (*Goes on his knees.*)

GWENDOLEN: Of course I will, darling. How long you have been about it! I am afraid you have had very little experience in how to propose.

JACK: My own one, I have never loved anyone in the world but you.

GWENDOLEN: Yes, but men often propose for practice. I know my brother Gerald does. All my girl-friends tell me so. What wonderfully blue eyes you have, Ernest! They are quite, quite, blue. I hope you will always look at me just like that, especially when there are other people present.

CANDIDA (1895)

by George Bernard Shaw

MARCHBANKS is an intense young poet of eighteen who has attached himself to the household of a preacher, James Morell. MARCHBANKS is in love with Mrs Morell, the 'Candida' of the title. PROSERPINE GARNETT, a few years older, is Rev Morell's secretary, who is secretly in love with her employer. MARCHBANKS has just been speaking about love.

Act II

PROSERPINE: Look here: if you don't stop talking like this, I'll leave the room, Mr Marchbanks: I really will. It's not proper. (*She resumes her seat at the typewriter, opening the blue book and preparing to copy a passage from it.*)

MARCHBANKS: (*Hopelessly.*) Nothing that's worth saying IS proper. (*He rises, and wanders about the room in his lost way, saying.*) I can't understand you, Miss Garnett. What am I to talk about?

PROSERPINE: (*Snubbing him.*) Talk about indifferent things, talk about the weather.

MARCHBANKS: Would you stand and talk about indifferent things if a child were by, crying bitterly with hunger?

PROSERPINE: I suppose not.

MARCHBANKS: Well: I can't talk about indifferent things with my heart crying out bitterly in ITS hunger.

PROSERPINE: Then hold your tongue.

MARCHBANKS: Yes: that is what it always comes to. We hold our tongues. Does that stop the cry of your heart? – for it does cry: doesn't it? It must, if you have a heart.

PROSERPINE: (*Suddenly rising with her hand pressed on her heart.*) Oh, it's no use trying to work while you talk like that. (*She leaves her little table and sits on the sofa. Her feelings are evidently strongly worked on.*) It's no business of yours, whether my heart cries or not; but I have a mind to tell you, for all that.

MARCHBANKS: You needn't. I know already that it must.

PROSERPINE: But mind: if you ever say I said so, I'll deny it.

MARCHBANKS: (*Compassionately.*) Yes, I know. And so you haven't the courage to tell him?

PROSERPINE: (*Bouncing up.*) HIM! Who?

MARCHBANKS: Whoever he is. The man you love. It might be anybody. The curate, Mr Mill, perhaps.

PROSERPINE: (*With disdain.*) Mr Mill!!! A fine man to break my heart about, indeed! I'd rather have you than Mr Mill.

MARCHBANKS: (*Recoiling.*) No, really – I'm very sorry; but you mustn't think of that. I –

PROSERPINE: (*Testily, crossing to the fire and standing at it with her back to him.*) Oh, don't be frightened: it's not you. It's not any one particular person.

MARCHBANKS: I know. You feel that you could love anybody that offered –

PROSERPINE: (*Exasperated.*) Anybody that offered! No, I do not. What do you take me for?

MARCHBANKS: (*Discouraged.*) No use. You won't make me REAL answers – only those things that everybody says. (*He strays to the sofa and sits down disconsolately.*)

PROSERPINE: (*Nettled at what she takes to be a disparagement of her manners by an aristocrat.*) Oh, well, if you want original conversation, you'd better go and talk to yourself.

MARCHBANKS: That is what all poets do: they talk to themselves out loud; and the world overhears them. But it's horribly lonely not to hear someone else talk sometimes.

PROSERPINE: Wait until Mr Morell comes. HE'LL talk to you.

(*MARCHBANKS shudders.*)

Oh, you needn't make wry faces over him: he can talk better than you. (*With temper.*) He'd talk your little head off.

(*She is going back angrily to her place, when, suddenly enlightened, he springs up and stops her.*)

MARCHBANKS: Ah, I understand now!

PROSERPINE: (*Reddening.*) What do you understand?

MARCHBANKS: Your secret. Tell me: is it really and

truly possible for a woman to love him?

PROSERPINE: (*As if this were beyond all bounds.*)
Well!!

MARCHBANKS: (*Passionately.*) No, answer me. I
want to know: I MUST know. I can't understand it. I
can see nothing in him but words, pious resolutions,
what people call goodness. You can't love that.

PROSERPINE: (*Attempting to snub him by an air of
cool propriety.*) I simply don't know what you're
talking about. I don't understand you.

MARCHBANKS: (*Vehemently.*) You do. You lie –

PROSERPINE: Oh!

MARCHBANKS: You DO understand; and you KNOW.
(*Determined to have an answer.*) Is it possible for a
woman to love him?

PROSERPINE: (*Looking him straight in the face.*)
Yes.

THE SEAGULL (1896)

by Anton Chekhov
Version by Peter Gill

PUBLISHED BY OBERON BOOKS (ISBN 1 84002 150 0)

*KONSTANTIN is an intense and passionate young man,
an aspiring writer. His mother, a celebrated actress, has
had an affair with a more successful writer, Trigorin.
KONSTANTIN and NINA once loved one another but
NINA was dazzled by Trigorin's charm and worldliness.
Trigorin had an affair with NINA, leaving her pregnant.
She became an actress. KONSTANTIN began to have
some success as a writer. In this scene, in the final act,
NINA and KONSTANTIN meet again after all these
events, sadder and older. Trigorin and KONSTANTIN's
mother have resumed their affair – he is in the next room.
It is a stormy night. KONSTANTIN, trying to write, hears
something outside. He opens the French windows to
discover NINA.*

Act IV

KONSTANTIN: What's that? (*Looking out of the
window.*) I can't see anything. (*Opening the French
window and looking into the garden.*) Someone ran
down the steps. (*Calls.*) Who's there?

(*He exits, then can be seen walking quickly along
the veranda. He returns half a minute later with NINA.
NINA lays her head on his chest and sobs quietly.*)

(*Moved.*) Nina. Nina, it's you. I had a feeling you
would come. I was right. I knew it. I've been restless
all day. My dear. My darling one. Don't cry. Don't.

NINA: There's someone there.

KONSTANTIN: No. No.

NINA: Lock the doors or someone will come in.

KONSTANTIN: No one will come in.

NINA: I know Irina Nikolaevna is here. Lock the doors.

> (*KONSTANTIN goes to the right-hand door and locks it and then goes over to the left-hand door.*)

KONSTANTIN: This one has no lock. I'll use a chair. (*Putting an armchair against the door.*) Don't be afraid, no one will come in now.

NINA: (*Looking into his face.*) Let me look at you. (*Looking around.*) How warm and nice it is in here. This used to be the drawing room. Have I changed much?

KONSTANTIN: Yes. You're thinner and your eyes seem bigger. Nina, you don't know how strange it is to see you again. Why wouldn't you see me? Why haven't you come here before this? I know you've been here for nearly a week. I've been to see you every day. Several times a day. I stood under the window like a beggar.

NINA: I was afraid that you hated me. Every night I've dreamt that you saw me but didn't recognise me. If only you knew. I've been coming here to the lake since the moment I arrived. I've been close to this house many times but I couldn't come in. Can we sit down?

> (*NINA and KONSTANTIN sit.*)

Let's sit down and talk and talk. It's nice here, so
warm and comfortable. Can you hear the wind?
There's a passage in Turgenev: 'Lucky is he who, on a
night like this, has a roof over his head and a warm
corner to sit in.' I'm a seagull. No. That's not it.
(*Rubbing her forehead.*) What was I saying? Oh
yes. Turgenev. 'May the Lord help all homeless
wanderers.' Never mind. (*Sobs.*)

KONSTANTIN: Nina. Don't cry, Nina.

NINA: Never mind. It does me good. I haven't cried for
two years. Late last evening I went to see if our
theatre was still there. When I saw it was still
standing, I cried for the first time in two years and felt
better for it. My mind was easier. I felt such relief.
You see, I'm not crying now. (*Taking him by the
hand.*) So you have become a writer then, is that so?
You're a writer and I'm an actress. We are both
caught up in it all. I used to be so happy. Like a child I
was so happy. I would wake up in the morning and I
would sing. I loved you. I dreamt of fame. And now?
Well, early tomorrow morning I have to travel third
class to Yelets with the peasants. Third class. And in
Yelets tradesmen with pretensions to culture will
pester me with their attentions. How sordid life is.

KONSTANTIN: Why are you going to Yelets?

NINA: I've taken an engagement there for the winter. I
should go.

KONSTANTIN: I cursed you, Nina. I hated you. I tore
up all your letters and photographs. But I knew all the
time that my soul was bound to you for ever. I can't
stop loving you. I haven't the strength. Ever since I

lost you, ever since they started publishing me, my life has been unbearable. I'm so unhappy. My youth has been taken from me. It's gone. They've stolen it. And I feel as if I've been living on the earth for ninety years. I call out your name, Nina. I've kissed the ground on which you walked. I can see your face wherever I look. Your kind smile that lit up the best years of my life.

NINA: (*Bewildered.*) Why is he talking like this?

KONSTANTIN: I'm so lonely with no one to warm me. I'm cold, as cold as if I was living in a cellar. Everything I write is dry, stale, miserable. Stay here with me, Nina. Or let me come with you.

(*NINA quickly puts on her hat and cape.*)

Nina, where are you going, for God's sake? Nina? (*Watches her get dressed.*)

(*Pause.*)

NINA: My horses are waiting at the gate. Don't see me out. I'll manage by myself. (*Through tears.*) Can I have some water?

KONSTANTIN: (*Giving her a drink of water.*) Where are you going?

NINA: Into town. (*Pause.*) Is Irina Nikolaevna here?

KONSTANTIN: Yes. My uncle was taken ill on Thursday so we telegraphed for her to come.

NINA: Why did you say that you kissed the ground on which I walked? I ought to be killed. (*Leaning over the table.*) I'm so tired. If only I could rest. If I could only rest.

BLOOD WEDDING (1933)

by Federico Garcia Lorca
Translated by Gwynne Edwards

PUBLISHED BY METHUEN (ISBN 0 413 15780 6)

This brief, poetic and bloody tragedy explores the profound and direct passions of Spanish peasant life. On her wedding day, a BRIDE jilts her groom and runs off with her former lover, LEONARDO. The bridegroom pursues them into the forest, determined to get his revenge. In this verse scene, the BRIDE and LEONARDO have just arrived in the forest, at dead of night.

Act III, Scene I

LEONARDO: Quiet!

BRIDE: I'll go on my own from here.
    You leave me! I want you to turn back.

LEONARDO: I said be quiet!

BRIDE: With your teeth,
    With your hands, any way you can,
    Tear the metal of this chain
    From my pure throat,
    And leave me locked away
    Here in my house of earth.
    And if you don't want to kill me
    As you'd kill a tiny viper,
    Put the barrel of your gun
    In these bride's hands of mine.
    Oh, what sorrow, what fire
    Sweeps upward through my head!

What splinters of glass are stuck in my tongue!

LEONARDO: We've taken the step; quiet!
    They are close behind us
    And I'm taking you with me.

BRIDE: It will have to be by force!

LEONARDO: By force? Who was it went
    Down the stairs first?

BRIDE: I did.

LEONARDO: Who was it put
    A fresh bridle on the horse?

BRIDE: I did. It's true.

LEONARDO: Which hands
    Strapped the spurs to my boots?

BRIDE: These hands, that are yours,
    That when they see you want
    To break the blue branches
    And the whisper of your veins.
    I love you! I love you! Leave me!
    For if I could kill you,
    I'd place a shroud over you
    Edged with violet.
    Oh, what sorrow, what fire
    Sweeps upward through my head!

LEONARDO: What splinters of glass are stuck in my tongue!
    Because I wanted to forget
    And I put a wall of stone
    Between your house and mine.
    It's the truth. Don't you remember?
    And when I saw you from far away

I threw sand in my eyes.
But I'd get on the horse
And the horse would go to your door.
And then the silver wedding-pins
Turned my red blood black,
And our dream began to fill
My flesh with poisonous weeds.
Oh, I'm not the one at fault.
The fault belongs to the earth
And that scent that comes
From your breasts and your hair.

BRIDE: Oh, there's no reason! I don't want
Your blood or your table,
And there's not a minute of the day
That I don't want to be with you,
Because you drag me and I come,
And you tell me to go back
And I follow you through the air
Like a blade of grass.
I've left a good man
And all his family
In the middle of my wedding,
And wearing my bride's crown.
The punishment will fall on you,
And I don't want it to happen.
Leave me here! You go!
No one will defend you.

LEONARDO: Birds of early morning
Are waking in the trees.
The night is slowly dying
On the sharp edge of the stone.
Let's go to a dark corner
Where I can always love you

For to me people don't matter,
Nor the poison they pour on us.

(*He embraces her strongly.*)

BRIDE: And I will sleep at your feet
And watch over your dreams.
Naked, looking at the fields,
(*Powerfully.*) As if I were a bitch.
Because that's what I am! Oh, I look at you
And your beauty burns me.

LEONARDO: Flame is fired by flame.
And the same small flame
Can kill two ears of grain together.
Come on!

(*He pulls her.*)

BRIDE: Where are you taking me?

LEONARDO: To a place where they can't go,
These men who are all around us.
Where I can look at you!

BRIDE: (*Sarcastically.*) Take me from fair to fair,
An insult to decent women,
So that people can see me
With my wedding sheets displayed
On the breeze, like banners.

LEONARDO: I want to leave you too,
If I thought as I ought to think.
But I go where you go.
And you too. Take a step. See.
Nails of moonlight join us,
My waist and your hips.

(*The whole scene is very strong, full of a great sensuality.*)

BRIDE: Listen!

LEONARDO: Someone's coming.

BRIDE: Go quickly!
    It's right that I should die here,
    My feet deep in the water
    And thorns stuck in my head.
    And let the leaves weep for me,
    A woman lost and virgin.

LEONARDO: Be quiet! They are coming up.

BRIDE: Go!

LEONARDO: Quiet! Don't let them hear us.
    You go first! Come on! Listen!

(*The Bride hesitates.*)

BRIDE: Both of us!

LEONARDO: (*Embracing her.*) Whatever you want!
    If they separate us, it will be
    Because I am dead.

BRIDE: I will be dead too.

(*They leave embracing each other.*)

DONA ROSITA THE SPINSTER (1935)

by Federico Garcia Lorca
Translated by Gwynne Edwards

PUBLISHED BY METHUEN (ISBN 0 413 15780 6)

ROSITA, an orphan, lives with her Aunt. A teenager, she is betrothed to the NEPHEW, who is about to leave for America to make his fortune. In this verse scene, they declare their love but the NEPHEW will soon betray ROSITA.

Act I

ROSITA: When your eyes met mine, cousin,
    They did so treacherously.
    When your hands gave me flowers, cousin,
    They did so deceitfully.
    And now, still young, you are leaving me
    To the nightingale's sad song.
    You, whom I loved so truly,
    Can only do me this wrong.
    How can you leave me so cruelly,
    Like the strings of a lute struck dumb?

NEPHEW: (*Taking her to the 'vis-à-vis' where they sit down.*) To me your love's precious, cousin,
    More precious than any gold.
    As the nightingale's silent in winter,
    You must resist imagined cold.
    There's no coldness in my going,
    Though my journey's across the sea,
    And the sea offers consolation,
    A quiet tranquillity
    That offers me salvation,
    Should passion seek to destroy me.

ROSITA: One night on my jasmine balcony
　　I lay asleep and dreaming,
　　And dreamt I saw two cherubs attend
　　A rose sick with yearning.
　　Her colour was the palest white,
　　But she turned the deepest red.
　　By nature fragile and tender,
　　Her burning petals bled,
　　Till, wounded by love's assault,
　　The rose lay cold and dead.
　　So I, innocent cousin,
　　In the garden of myrtle walking,
　　To the fountain offered my paleness,
　　To the soft wind my longing.
　　Like a tender, foolish gazelle,
　　I dared to look on you lovingly,
　　At once my heart was pierced
　　By needles of quivering agony.
　　Its wounds as red as wallflower
　　Began to bleed fatally.

NEPHEW: Cousin, I shall come back to you,
　　I give you my word truly,
　　In a boat fashioned of gold,
　　Its sails guided by loyalty.
　　In sun and shadow, night and day,
　　I shall dream of you faithfully.

ROSITA: When the spirit's left alone,
　　Love drips its poison slowly.
　　With earth and salt it shall weave
　　The shroud that will soon clothe me.

NEPHEW: When my horse stops to graze
　　On the grass wet with dew,
　　When the mist lies on the river,

And the wall of the wind's white through,
When the burning heat of summer
Scorches the blood-red plain,
And the frost's starry needles
Are a bright stab of pain.
Then I will make my promise
And never leave you again.

ROSITA: My dream is to see you come, cousin,
At night through Granada to me,
When the light's full of salt, cousin,
From longing for the sea.
A lemon grove of yellow,
Jasmine that's white and bloodless,
Stones that kill with their hardness,
All will stop your progress,
And nards spinning like whirlpools
Will fill my house with madness.
Will you ever come back?

NEPHEW: I promise.

ROSITA: What dove shall I look for, anxiously,
To bring me news of your coming?

NEPHEW: The dove that stands for my loyalty.

ROSITA: Then I for the two of us
Will embroider the whitest sheets.

NEPHEW: In Jesus's name, his diamond crown,
The red carnation of his side and feet,
I promise I shall come back again.

ROSITA: God go with you, cousin!

NEPHEW: God be with you, till we meet again!

III: FEMALE / FEMALE DUOLOGUES

ANTIGONE (442 BC)

by Sophocles
English version by Declan Donnellan

PUBLISHED BY OBERON BOOKS (ISBN 1 84002 136 5)

The two sons of the banished King Oedipus led a failed
rebellion against the tyrannical Creon, King of Thebes.
Both were killed, and Creon has given orders that their
bodies should remain unburied. In Greek terms, this
means that they cannot pass on to the afterlife. However,
their sister ANTIGONE has crept out on to the battlefield
before dawn and tells her sister, ISMENE, what she has
done.

ANTIGONE: Ismene, my sister, my soul. Can you
 Believe that Zeus has found new pain for us?
 Oedipus' little girls must weep again.
 His inventiveness knows no bounds. New sins,
 New shames, new stains all tumble on our heads.
 Now this edict proclaimed to the city
 By our new leader. Have you heard nothing?
 Great evil hurtles at someone we love.

ISMENE: Not a word, Antigone, not a word,
 Since they came and said our brothers were dead,
 And how they'd murdered each other with swords
 And that now it is only you and me.
 I swear I've seen nothing since the Argives
 Limped away last night, nothing anyway
 That could make things either better or worse.

ANTIGONE: Just what I suspected: you know nothing.
 I sent for you to come outside for only
 You must hear what I'm about to say.

ISMENE: What is it? Tell me! You're frightening me.

ANTIGONE: Our brothers' bodies, Ismene.
  Creon has decided to honour one
  And shame the other. So Eteocles
  Lies in state, while hymns wing him to the Gods,
  The wails and moans and prayers of sobbing Thebes
  Echo round his senseless ears, but silent
  Lies the corpse of unheard Polynices.
  Nor man, nor woman, nor child may weep for him.
  Only the yellow wind and wild hyena
  Sing for him beyond the walls, and sightless
  His tender smile is dug by birds, who eye
  And mock his outstretched nakedness.
  He has decreed this to me, Ismene,
  He has decreed this to you, and is about
  To decree this to the entire city.
  He will make one thing absolutely clear:
  Good uncle Creon will not tolerate
  Any infraction of his mighty law.
  The punishment is death: public stoning,
  I believe. So Ismene, there you are.
  It's all up to you: are you a coward?
  Or born of a great father and mother?

ISMENE: But Antigone, what good can I do?

ANTIGONE: It's up to you to join me in my struggle.

ISMENE: What are you talking about? What struggle?

ANTIGONE: Will you help me move our brother's body?

ISMENE: What, are you going to try to bury him?
  You've just told me that it's against the law.

ANTIGONE: If you don't help me I'll do it alone.
  I won't be seen to betray our brother.

ISMENE: You're quite mad, Creon has forbidden it.

ANTIGONE: Creon cannot split me from my brother.

ISMENE: Oh no? Think about it, Antigone.
Our father died notorious and shamed.
He saw his crimes and never saw again,
Never saw his eyes twitching in his palms.
But we could see, Antigone, we saw
Our mother, Jocasta, his mother-wife,
Twist silently at the end of a rope.
Our brothers saw the bright crown fall and roll,
They killed each other while it rattled round,
And now it only stirs when Creon nods.
If we two break his law, what punishments
Will spill upon the daughters of Oedipus?
No, Antigone, now we're all that's left,
And must remember that we're only women.
We can't fight men! The king is powerful,
We are weak and must learn to bear with patience
The pain that is, and was, and that will come.
I beg those beneath the earth to understand
I have no choice but to obey authority.
Sometimes it is prudent to compromise.

ANTIGONE: I can hardly order you, Ismene,
But hear this: even when you change your mind
And beg me on your knees to sacrifice
Yourself in glory, it will be too late.
Sister: be whoever you want to be,
Be who you think best, but I will bury him.
It is a fine thing for me to die like this;
Brother and sister shall lie together.
This crime is holy, it shuffles me off
To Hades, where father, mother, brother
Count the breaths I waste in Thebes. You must do

Whatever seems right, Ismene, you choose,
If it really seems right to dishonour
The will of the Gods.

ISMENE: You know I'd never dishonour the Gods
But I cannot defy the city.

ANTIGONE: No.
You make all the excuses you can but
I'll bury my brother with dignity.

ISMENE: You make my blood run cold, Antigone.

ANTIGONE: Do not fear for me. Look out for yourself.

ISMENE: Promise me at least you won't tell a soul.
Keep it a secret and I'll do the same.

ANTIGONE: Oh no, Ismene, tell everybody –
Yell it to Thebes. Scream it from seven gates!

ISMENE: You have wild eyes, I don't know you
anymore.

ANTIGONE: I know who I am. And I also know
My family sees I am doing right.

ISMENE: You think you'll take a spade and dig the grave
All by yourself? You'll never have the strength.

ANTIGONE: I'll take a rest when I run out of breath.

ISMENE: It is wrong to seek the impossible.

ANTIGONE: Go on, Ismene, if you want my hate;
If Polynices hears, he'll hate you too.
Just go, and let me do my foolery.
I'd rather kneel as marble till their stones
Bludgeon me to softness, than yield to him
And live in decent shame.

ISMENE: You must do whatever seems right to you.
　　　All I can say is this: I think you're mad.
　　　But you will always be loved, Antigone.

　　(*Exeunt ANTIGONE and ISMENE.*)

HENRY VIII (1612)

by William Shakespeare and John Fletcher

This late collaboration by Shakespeare tells the story of Katherine of Aragon, Henry's first wife, with considerable sympathy. Her successor, ANNE BOLEYN (or Bullen), plays a relatively small part in the action. In this slightly adapted scene, ANNE is seen at court with an OLD LADY, a fellow lady-in-waiting to the Queen.

ANNE: Not for that, neither: here's the pang that pinches:
    His highness having lived so long with her, and she
    So good a lady that no tongue could ever
    Pronounce dishonour of her – by my life,
    She never knew harm-doing – O, now, after
    So many courses of the sun enthroned,
    Still growing in a majesty and pomp, the which
    To leave a thousand-fold more bitter than
    'Tis sweet at first to acquire – after this process,
    To give her the avaunt! It is a pity
    Would move a monster.

OLD LADY: Hearts of most hard temper
    Melt and lament for her.

ANNE: O, God's will! Much better
    She ne'er had known pomp: though't be temporal,
    Yet if that quarrel, fortune, do divorce
    It from the bearer, 'tis a sufferance panging
    As soul and body's severing.

OLD LADY: Alas, poor lady,
    She's a stranger now again.

ANNE: So much the more
Must pity drop upon her. Verily,
I swear, 'tis better to be lowly born,
And range with humble livers in content,
Than to be perk'd up in a glistering grief
And wear a golden sorrow.

OLD LADY: Our content
Is our best having.

ANNE: By my troth and maidenhead,
I would not be a queen.

OLD LADY: Beshrew me, I would,
And venture maidenhead for't; and so would you,
For all this spice of your hypocrisy:
You, that have so fair parts of woman on you,
Have too a woman's heart; which ever yet
Affected eminence, wealth, sovereignty;
Which, to say sooth, are blessings; and which gifts –
Saving your mincing – the capacity
Of your soft cheveril conscience would receive
If you might please to stretch it.

ANNE: Nay, good troth.

OLD LADY: Yes, troth, and troth; you would not be a
                                                              queen?

ANNE: No, not for all the riches under heaven.

OLD LADY: 'Tis strange; a threepence bawd would hire me,
     Old as I am, to queen it: but, I pray you,
     What think you of a duchess? Have you limbs
     To bear that load of title?

ANNE: No, in truth.

OLD LADY: Then you are weakly made: pluck off a little;
     I would not be a young count in your way,

For more than blushing comes to: if your back
Cannot vouchsafe this burden, 'tis too weak
Ever to get a boy.

ANNE: How you do talk!
I swear again, I would not be a queen
For all the world.

OLD LADY: In faith, for little England
You'd venture an emballing: I myself
Would for Carnarvonshire, although there 'long'd
No more to the crown but that. But look you here.

(*Hands ANNE a letter.*)

The king's majesty
Commends his good opinion of you, and
Does purpose honour to you no less flowing
Than Marchioness of Pembroke; to which title
A thousand pound a year, annual support,
Out of his grace he adds.

ANNE: (*After reading.*)   I do not know
What kind of obedience I should tender;
More than my all is nothing: nor my prayers
Are not words duly hallowed, nor my wishes
More worth than empty vanities; yet prayers and
                                        wishes
Are all I can return.

OLD LADY: Why, this it is; see, see!
I have been begging sixteen years in court
Am yet a courtier beggarly, nor could
Come pat betwixt too early and too late
For any suit of pounds; and you, O fate!
A very fresh fish here – fie, fie, fie upon
This compell'd fortune! – have your mouth fill'd up
Before you open it.

ANNE: This is strange to me.

OLD LADY: How tastes it? Is it bitter? Forty pence, no.
There was a lady once, 'tis an old story,
That would not be a queen, that would she not,
For all the mud in Egypt; have you heard it?

ANNE: Come, you are pleasant.

OLD LADY: With your theme, I could
O'ermount the lark. The Marchioness of Pembroke!
A thousand pounds a year for pure respect!
No other obligation! By my life,
That promises more thousands: honour's train
Is longer than his foreskirt. By this time
I know your back will bear a duchess: say,
Are you not stronger than you were?

ANNE: Good lady,
Make yourself mirth with your particular fancy,
And leave me out of it. Would I had no being,
If this salute my blood a jot: it faints me,
To think what follows.
The queen is comfortless, and we forgetful
In our long absence: pray, do not deliver
What here you've heard to her.

OLD LADY: What do you think me?

(*They exit.*)

THE GENTLEMAN DANCING MASTER (1671)

by William Wycherley

HIPPOLITA is fifteen, romantic and extremely curious about men. However, she has been confined to the house by her father and her aunt, and has only her maid, PRUE, for company. Here they complain about their cruel treatment and attempt to plot their way out of it.

Act I, Scene I

Enter HIPPOLITA and PRUE her Maid.

HIPPOLITA: To confine a Woman just in her rambling Age! take away her liberty at the very time she shou'd use it! O barbarous Aunt! O unnatural Father! to shut up a poor Girl at fourteen, and hinder her budding; all things are ripen'd by the Sun; to shut up a poor Girl at fourteen!

PRUE: 'Tis true, Miss, two poor young Creatures as we are!

HIPPOLITA: Not suffer'd to see a play in a twelve-month!

PRUE: Nor to go to Ponchinello nor Paradise!

HIPPOLITA: Nor to take a Ramble to the Park nor Mulberry-gar'n!

PRUE: Nor to Tatnam-Court nor Islington!

HIPPOLITA: Nor to eat a Sillybub in new Spring-gar'n with a Cousin!

PRUE: Nor to drink a pint of Wine with a Friend at the Prince in the Sun!

HIPPOLITA: Nor to hear a Fiddle in good Company.

PRUE: Nor to hear the Organs and Tongs at the Gun in Moorfields!

HIPPOLITA: Nay, not suffer'd to go to Church, because the men are sometimes there! little did I think I should ever have long'd to go to Church!

PRUE: Or I either, but between two Maids!

HIPPOLITA: Not see a man!

PRUE: Nor come near a man!

HIPPOLITA: Nor hear of a man

PRUE: No, Miss, but to be deny'd a man! and to have no use at all of a man!

HIPPOLITA: Hold, hold – your resentment is as much greater than mine, as your experience has been greater; but all this while, what do we make of my Cousin, my Husband elect (as my Aunt says) we have had his Company these three days. Is he no man?

PRUE: No faith, he's but a Monsieur, but you'll resolve your self that question within these three days: for by that time, he'll be your Husband, if your Father come to night?

HIPPOLITA: Or if I provide not my self with another in the mean time! For Fathers seldom chuse well, and I will no more take my Fathers choice in a Husband, than I would in a Gown or a Suit of Knots: so that if that Cousin of mine were not an ill contriv'd ugly-Freekish-fool, in being my Fathers choice, I shou'd hate him; besides, he has almost made me out of love with mirth and good humour, for he debases it as much as a Jack-pudding; and Civility and good Breeding more than a City Dancing-Master.

PRUE: What, won't you marry him then, Madam?

HIPPOLITA: Wou'dst thou have me marry a Fool! an Idiot?

PRUE: Lord! 'tis a sign you have been kept up indeed! and know little of the World to refuse a man for a Husband, only because he's a Fool. Methinks he's a pretty apish kind of a Gentleman, like other Gentlemen, and handsom enough to lye with in the dark; when Husbands take their priviledges, and for the day-times you may take the priviledge of a Wife.

HIPPOLITA: Excellent Governess, you do understand the World, I see.

PRUE: Then you shou'd be guided by me.

HIPPOLITA: Art thou in earnest then, damn'd Jade? wou'dst thou have me marry him? well – there are more poor young Women undone and married to filthy Fellows, by the treachery and evil counsel of Chamber-maids, than by the obstinacy and covetousness of Parents.

PRUE: Does not your Father come on purpose out of Spain to marry you to him? Can you release your self from your Aunt or Father any other way? Have you a mind to be shut up as long as you live? For my part (though you can hold out upon the Lime from the Walls here, Salt, old Shoes, and Oat-meal) I cannot live so, I must confess my patience is worn out.

HIPPOLITA: Alas! alas! poor Prue! your stomach lies another way, I will take pity of you, and get me a Husband very suddenly, who may have a Servant at your service; but rather than marry my Cousin, I will be a Nun in the new Protestant Nunnery they talk of, where (they say) there will be no hopes of coming near a man.

PRUE: But you can marry no body but your Cousin, Miss, your Father you expect to night, and be certain his Spanish policy and wariness, which has kept you up so close ever since you came from Hackney-School, will make sure of you within a day or two at farthest.

HIPPOLITA: Then 'tis time to think how to prevent him – stay –

PRUE: In vain, vain Miss!

HIPPOLITA: If we knew but any man, any man, though he were but a little handsomer than the Devil, so that he were a Gentleman.

PRUE: What if you did know any man, if you had an opportunity; cou'd you have confidence to speak to a man first? But if you cou'd, how cou'd you come to him, or he to you? nay how cou'd you send to him? for though you cou'd write, which your Father in his Spanish prudence wou'd never permit you to learn, who shou'd carry the Letter? but we need not be concern'd for that, since we know not to whom to send it.

HIPPOLITA: Stay! – it must be so – I'le try however.

THE COUNTRY WIFE (1672)

by William Wycherley

ALITHEA and her plain-speaking maid LUCY almost come to blows in this significant scene from the sub-plot of Wycherley's most famous comedy. ALITHEA, a young woman of quality, is about to give herself to Sparkish when she (and LUCY) knows that she is truly in love with Harcourt.

Act. IV, Scene I

Enter ALITHEA dressed in new clothes, and LUCY.

LUCY: Well – madam, now have I dressed you, and set you out with so many ornaments, and spent upon you ounces of essence and pulvillio; and all this for no other purpose but as people adorn and perfume a corpse for a stinking second-hand grave: such, or as bad, I think Master Sparkish's bed.

ALITHEA: Hold your peace.

LUCY: Nay, madam, I will ask you the reason why you would banish poor Master Harcourt for ever from your sight; how could you be so hard-hearted?

ALITHEA: 'Twas because I was not hard-hearted.

LUCY: No, no; 'twas stark love and kindness, I warrant.

ALITHEA: It was so; I would see him no more because I love him.

LUCY: Hey day, a very pretty reason!

ALITHEA: You do not understand me.

LUCY: I wish you may yourself.

ALITHEA: I was engaged to marry, you see, another man, whom my justice will not suffer me to deceive or injure.

LUCY: Can there be a greater cheat or wrong done to a man than to give him your person without your heart? I should make a conscience of it.

ALITHEA: I'll retrieve it for him after I am married a while.

LUCY: The woman that marries to love better, will be as much mistaken as the wencher that marries to live better. No, madam, marrying to increase love is like gaming to become rich; alas! you only lose what little stock you had before.

ALITHEA: I find by your rhetoric you have been bribed to betray me.

LUCY: Only by his merit, that has bribed your heart, you see, against your word and rigid honour. But what a devil is this honour! 'tis sure a disease in the head, like the megrim or falling-sickness, that always hurries people away to do themselves mischief. Men lose their lives by it; women, what's dearer to 'em, their love, the life of life.

ALITHEA: Come, pray talk you no more of honour, nor Master Harcourt; I wish the other would come to secure my fidelity to him and his right in me.

LUCY: You will marry him then?

ALITHEA: Certainly, I have given him already my word, and will my hand too, to make it good, when he comes.

LUCY: Well, I wish I may never stick pin more, if he be not an arrant natural, to t'other fine gentleman.

ALITHEA: I own he wants the wit of Harcourt, which I will dispense withal for another want he has, which is want of jealousy, which men of wit seldom want.

LUCY: Lord, madam, what should you do with a fool to your husband? You intend to be honest, don't you? then that husbandly virtue, credulity, is thrown away upon you.

ALITHEA: He only that could suspect my virtue should have cause to do it; 'tis Sparkish's confidence in my truth that obliges me to be so faithful to him.

LUCY: You are not sure his opinion may last.

ALITHEA: I am satisfied, 'tis impossible for him to be jealous after the proofs I have had of him. Jealousy in a husband – Heaven defend me from it! it begets a thousand plagues to a poor woman, the loss of her honour, her quiet, and her –

LUCY: And her pleasure.

ALITHEA: What d'ye mean, impertinent?

LUCY: Liberty is a great pleasure, madam.

ALITHEA: I say, loss of her honour, her quiet, nay, her life sometimes; and what's as bad almost, the loss of this town; that is, she is sent into the country, which is the last ill-usage of a husband to a wife, I think.

LUCY: (*Aside*.) O, does the wind lie there? – (*Aloud*.) Then of necessity, madam, you think a man must carry his wife into the country, if he be wise. The country is as terrible, I find, to our young English ladies, as a monastery to those abroad; and on my virginity, I think they would rather marry a London jailer, than a high sheriff of a county, since neither can stir from his employment. Formerly women of wit married fools for a great estate, a fine seat, or the like; but now 'tis for a pretty seat only in Lincoln's Inn Fields, St. James's Fields, or the Pall Mall.

THE RECRUITING OFFICER (1706)

by George Farquhar

MELINDA and SILVIA were brought up together in Shrewsbury. SILVIA is the daughter of the local magistrate and a feisty, independent-minded young woman. MELINDA's financial circumstances were strained. She fell in love with Worthy, a local citizen, but could bring no dowry to the marriage. She was prepared to entertain an offer from Worthy to receive a generous allowance in return for being his mistress. However, before this plan was put into action, MELINDA inherited a fortune and has now become rather full of herself, spurning Worthy and patronising her friend. Here, SILVIA visits MELINDA after having been out of Shrewsbury for some time. SILVIA is in love with the rakish Captain Plume, the recruiting officer of the title, who has just returned to the town.

Act I, Scene II

MELINDA: Welcome to town, Cousin Silvia. (*Salute.*) I envy'd you your retreat in the country; for Shrewsbury, methinks, and all your heads of shires, are the most irregular places for living, here we have smoke, noise, scandal, affectation, and pretension; in short, every thing to give the spleen, and nothing to divert it – Then the air is intolerable.

SILVIA: Oh! madam, I have heard the town commended for its air.

MELINDA: But you don't consider, Silvia, how long I have liv'd in it; for I can assure you, that to a lady the least nice in her constitution, no air can be good above half a year; change of air I take to be the most agreeable of any variety in life.

SILVIA: As you say, cousin Melinda, there are several sorts of airs, airs in conversation, airs in behaviour, airs in dress; then we have our quality airs, our sickly airs, our reserv'd airs, and sometimes our impudent airs.

MELINDA: Pshaw – I talk only of the air we breathe, or more properly of that we taste. Have you not, Silvia, found a vast difference in the taste of airs?

SILVIA: Pray cousin, are not vapours a sort of air? Taste air! You may as well tell me I might feed upon air; but prithee, my dear Melinda, don't put on such airs to me, your education and mine were just the same, and I remember the time when we never troubled our heads about air, but when the sharp air from the Welsh mountains made our noses drop in a cold morning at the boarding-school.

MELINDA: Our education, cousin, was the same, but our temperaments had nothing alike; you have the constitution of a horse.

SILVIA: So far as to be troubled with neither spleen, colic, nor vapours, I need no salt for my stomach, no hart's-hom for my head, nor wash for my complexion; I can gallop all the morning after the hunting horn, and all the evening after a fiddle: In short, I can do every thing with my father but drink and shoot flying; and I'm sure I can do every thing my mother cou'd, were I put to the trial.

MELINDA: You're in a fair way of being put to't; for I'm told, your Captain is come to town.

SILVIA: Ay, Melinda, he is come, and I'll take care he shan't go without a companion.

MELINDA: You're certainly mad, cousin.

SILVIA: 'And there's a pleasure sure, in being mad; Which none but mad-men know.'[1]

MELINDA: Thou poor romantic Quixote, hast thou the vanity to imagine that a young sprightly officer that rambles over half the globe in half a year, can confine his thoughts to the little daughter of a country Justice in an obscure corner of the world?

SILVIA: Pshaw! What care I for his thoughts? I shou'd not like a man with confin'd thoughts, it shows a narrowness of soul. Constancy is but a dull, sleepy quality at best; they will hardly admit it among the manly virtues nor do I think it deserves a place with bravery, knowledge, policy, justice, and some other qualities that are proper to that noble sex. In short, Melinda, I think a petticoat a mighty simple thing, and I'm heartily tir'd of my sex.

MELINDA: That is, you are tir'd of an appendix to our sex that you can't so handsomely get rid of in petticoats as if you were in breeches – O' my conscience, Silvia, hadst thou been a man, thou hadst been the greatest rake in Christendom.

SILVIA: I shou'd endeavour to know the world, which a man can never do thoroughly without half a hundred friendships, and as many amours. But now I think on't, how stands your affair with Mr Worthy?

MELINDA: He's my aversion.

1 *'And there's...'* Silvia is quoting a popular song of the period

SILVIA: Vapours.

MELINDA: What do you say, madam?

SILVIA: I say, that you shou'd not use that honest fellow
so inhumanely, he's a gentleman of parts and fortune,
and beside that he's my Plume's friend; and by all
that's sacred, if you don't use him better, I shall expect
satisfaction.

MELINDA: Satisfaction! You begin to fancy your self in
breeches in good earnest – But to be plain with you, I
like Worthy the worse for being so intimate with your
captain; for I take him to be a loose, idle, unmannerly
coxcomb.

SILVIA: Oh! Madam – You never saw him, perhaps,
since you were mistress of twenty thousand pound;
you only knew him when you were capitulating with
Worthy for a settlement, which perhaps might
encourage him to be a little loose and unmannerly with
you.

MELINDA: What do you mean, madam?

SILVIA: My meaning needs no interpretation, madam.

MELINDA: Better it had, madam – for methinks you're
too plain.

SILVIA: If you mean the plainness of my person, I think
your Ladyship as plain as me to the full.

MELINDA: Were I assur'd of that, I shou'd be glad to
take up with a rakely officer as you do.

SILVIA: Again! Look'e, madam – You're in your own
house.

MELINDA: And if you had kept in yours, I shou'd have excus'd you.

SILVIA: Don't be troubl'd, madam – I shan't desire to have my visit return'd.

MELINDA: The sooner therefore you make an end of this, the better.

SILVIA: I'm easily advis'd to follow my inclinations – So madam – Your humble servant.

(*Exit SILVIA.*)

MELINDA: Saucy thing!

THE RIVALS (1775)

by Richard Brinsley Sheridan

Wealthy, flighty and romantic LYDIA LANGUISH is in Bath with her aunt and guardian, Mrs Malaprop. She is delighted to receive a visit from her dear friend JULIA MELVILLE, another well-placed young woman of marriageable age who is the ward of Sir Anthony Absolute. There is a plan, conceived and supported by Sir Anthony and Mrs Malaprop, that LYDIA should marry Sir Anthony's son, but she is in love elsewhere. JULIA, meanwhile, is in love with Faulkland, but there are obstacles in their way.

Act I, Scene II

LYDIA: My dearest Julia, how delighted am I! – (*Embrace.*) How unexpected was this happiness!

JULIA: True, Lydia – and our pleasure is the greater. – But what has been the matter? – you were denied to me at first!

LYDIA: Ah, Julia, I have a thousand things to tell you! – But first inform me what has conjured you to Bath? – Is Sir Anthony here?

JULIA: He is – we are arrived within this hour – and I suppose he will be here to wait on Mrs Malaprop as soon as he is dressed.

LYDIA: Then before we are interrupted, let me impart to you some of my distress! – I know your gentle nature will sympathize with me, though your prudence may condemn me! My letters have informed you of my whole connection with Beverley; but I have lost him,

Julia! My aunt has discovered our intercourse by a note she intercepted, and has confined me ever since! Yet, would you believe it? she has absolutely fallen in love with a tall Irish baronet she met one night since she has been here, at Lady Macshuffle's rout.

JULIA: You jest, Lydia!

LYDIA: No, upon my word. – She really carries on a kind of correspondence with him, under a feigned name though, till she chooses to be known to him: but it is a Delia or a Celia, I assure you.

JULIA: Then, surely, she is now more indulgent to her niece.

LYDIA: Quite the contrary. Since she has discovered her own frailty, she is become more suspicious of mine. Then I must inform you of another plague! That odious Acres is to be in Bath today: so that I protest I shall be teased out of all spirits!

JULIA: Come, come, Lydia, hope for the best – Sir Anthony shall use his interest with Mrs Malaprop.

LYDIA: But you have not heard the worst. Unfortunately I had quarrelled with my poor Beverley, just before my aunt made the discovery, and I have not seen him since to make it up.

JULIA: What was his offence?

LYDIA: Nothing at all! But, I don't know how it was, as often as we had been together, we had never had a quarrel, and, somehow, I was afraid he would never give me an opportunity. So, last Thursday, I wrote a letter to myself, to inform myself that Beverley was at that time paying his addresses to another woman. I signed it your friend unknown, showed it to Beverley, charged him with his falsehood, put myself in a violent passion, and vowed I'd never see him more.

JULIA: And you let him depart so, and have not seen him since?

LYDIA: 'Twas the next day my aunt found the matter out. I intended only to have teased him three days and a half, and now I've lost him for ever.

JULIA: If he is as deserving and sincere as you have represented him to me, he will never give you up so. Yet, consider, Lydia, you tell me he is but an ensign, and you have thirty thousand pounds.

LYDIA: But you know I loose most of my fortune if I marry without my aunt's consent, till of age; and that is what I have determined to do, ever since I knew the penalty. Nor could I love the man who would wish to wait a day for the alternative.

JULIA: Nay, this is caprice!

LYDIA: What, does Julia tax me with caprice? I thought her lover Faulkland had inured her to it.

JULIA: I do not love even his faults.

LYDIA: But apropos – you have sent to him, I suppose?

JULIA: Not yet, upon my word – nor has he the least idea of my being in Bath. Sir Anthony's resolution was so sudden, I could not inform him of it.

LYDIA: Well, Julia, you are your own mistress (though under the protection of Sir Anthony), yet have you, for this long year, been a slave to the caprice, the whim, the jealousy of this ungrateful Faulkland, who will ever delay assuming the right of a husband, while you suffer him to be equally imperious as a lover.

JULIA: Nay, you are wrong entirely. We were contracted before my father's death. That, and some consequent embarrassments, have delayed what I know to be my Faulkland's most ardent wish. He is too generous to trifle on such a point – and for his character, you wrong him there, too. No, Lydia, he is too proud, too noble, to be jealous; if he is captious, 'tis without dissembling; if fretful, without rudeness. Unused to the fopperies of love, he is negligent of the little duties expected from a lover – but being unhackneyed in the passion, his affection is ardent and sincere; and as it engrosses his whole soul, he expects every thought and emotion of his mistress to move in unison with his. Yet, though his pride calls for this full return, his humility makes him undervalue those qualities in him which would entitle him to it; and not feeling why he should be loved to the degree he wishes, he still suspects that he is not loved enough. This temper, I must own, has cost me many unhappy hours; but I have learned to think myself his debtor, for those imperfections which arise from the ardour of his attachment.

LYDIA: Well, I cannot blame you for defending him. But tell me candidly, Julia, had he never saved your life, do you think you should have been attached to him as you are? – Believe me, the rude blast that overset your boat was a prosperous gale of love to him.

JULIA: Gratitude may have strengthened my attachment to Mr Faulkland, but I loved him before he had preserved me; yet surely that alone were an obligation sufficient.

LYDIA: Obligation! why a water spaniel would have done as much! – Well, I should never think of giving my heart to a man because he could swim.

THE SCHOOL FOR SCANDAL (1777)

by Richard Brinsley Sheridan

*LADY SNEERWELL and her toadying companion, MISS
VERJUICE, are the leaders of a particularly vicious
group of gossip mongers in high society whose actions
greatly affect the reputations of all those who come to
their notice. It is morning in LADY SNEERWELL's house.
LADY SNEERWELL is at her dressing table with her maid,
Lappet, and MISS VERJUICE is drinking coffee.*

Act I, Scene I

LADY SNEERWELL: The paragraphs you say were all
    inserted:

VERJUICE: They were madam – and as I copied them
    myself in a feigned hand there can be no suspicion
    whence they came.

LADY SNEERWELL: Did you circulate the report of
    Lady Brittle's Intrigue with Captain Boastall?

VERJUICE: Madam by this time Lady Brittle is the talk
    of half the town – and I doubt not in a week the men
    will toast her as a demirep.

LADY SNEERWELL: What have you done as to the
    insinuation as to a certain Baronet's lady and a certain
    cook.

VERJUICE: That is in as fine a train as your Ladyship
    could wish. I told the story yesterday to my own maid
    with directions to communicate it directly to my
    hairdresser. He I am informed has a Brother who
    courts a milliners' prentice in Pallmall whose mistress

has a first cousin whose sister is *femme de chambre* to Mrs Clackit – so that in the common course of things it must reach Mrs Clackit's ears within four-and-twenty hours and then you know the business is as good as done.

LADY SNEERWELL: Why truly Mrs Clackit has a very pretty talent – a great deal of industry – yet – yes – been tolerably successful in her way – to my knowledge she has been the cause of breaking off six matches, of three sons being disinherited and four daughters being turned out of doors. Of three several elopements, as many close confinements – nine separate maintenances and two divorces – nay I have more than once traced her causing a tête-à-tête in the Town and Country magazine – when the parties perhaps had never seen each other's faces before in the course of their lives.

VERJUICE: She certainly has talents.

LADY SNEERWELL: But her manner is gross.

VERJUICE: 'Tis very true. She generally designs well, has a free tongue and a bold invention – but her colouring is too dark and her outline often extravagant – She wants that delicacy of tint – and mellowness of sneer – which distinguish your Ladyship's scandal.

LADY SNEERWELL: Ah you are partial Verjuice.

VERJUICE: Not in the least – everybody allows that Lady Sneerwell can do more with a word or a look than many can with the most laboured detail even when they happen to have a little truth on their side to support it.

LADY SNEERWELL: Yes my dear Verjuice. I am no hypocrite to deny the satisfaction I reap from the success of my efforts. Wounded myself, in the early part of my life by the envenomed tongue of slander I confess I have since known no pleasure equal to the reducing others to the level of my own injured reputation.

VERJUICE: Nothing can be more natural – But my dear Lady Sneerwell there is one affair in which you have lately employed me, wherein, I confess I am at a loss to guess your motives.

LADY SNEERWELL: I conceive you mean with respect to my neighbour, Sir Peter Teazle, and his family – Lappet. – And has my conduct in this matter really appeared to you so mysterious?

(*Exit MAID.*)

VERJUICE: Entirely so. An old bachelor as Sir Peter was, having taken a young wife from out of the country – as Lady Teazle is – are certainly fair subjects for a little mischievous raillery – but here are two young men – to whom Sir Peter has acted as a kind of guardian since their father's death, the eldest possessing the most amiable character and universally well spoken of, the youngest the most dissipated and extravagant young fellow in the kingdom, without friends or character – the former one an avowed admirer of yours and apparently your favourite, the latter attached to Maria Sir Peter's ward – and confessedly beloved by her. Now on the face of these circumstances it is utterly unaccountable to me why you a young widow with no great jointure – should not close with the passion of a man of such character and expectations as Mr Surface – and more so why you should be so uncommonly earnest to destroy the mutual Attachment subsisting between his Brother Charles and Maria.

LADY SNEERWELL: Then at once to unravel this mistery – I must inform you that love has no share whatever in the intercourse between Mr Surface and me.

VERJUICE: No!

LADY SNEERWELL: His real attachment is to Maria or her fortune – but finding in his brother a favoured rival, he has been obliged to mask his pretensions – and profit by my assistance.

VERJUICE: Yet still I am more puzzled why you should interest yourself in his success.

LADY SNEERWELL: Heavens! how dull you are! cannot you surmise the weakness which I hitherto, thro' shame have concealed even from you – must I confess that Charles – that libertine, that extravagant, that bankrupt in fortune and reputation – that he it is for whom I am thus anxious and malicious and to gain whom I would sacrifice – everything –

VERJUICE: Now indeed – your conduct appears consistent and I no longer wonder at your enmity to Maria, but how came you and Surface so confidential?

LADY SNEERWELL: For our mutual interest – but I have found out him a long time since, altho' he has contrived to deceive everybody beside – I know him to be artful selfish and malicious – while with Sir Peter, and indeed with all his acquaintance, he passes for a youthful miracle of prudence – good sense and benevolence.

VERJUICE: Yes yes – I know Sir Peter vows he has not his equal in England; and, above all, he praises him as a man of sentiment.

LADY SNEERWELL: True and with the assistance of his sentiments and hypocrisy he has brought Sir Peter entirely in his interests with respect to Maria and is now I believe attempting to flatter Lady Teazle into the same good opinion towards him – while poor Charles has no friend in the house – though I fear he has a powerful one in Maria's heart, against whom we must direct our schemes.

A DOLL'S HOUSE (1879)

by Henrik Ibsen
Translated by Michael Meyer

PUBLISHED BY METHUEN (ISBN 0 413 46340 0)

NORA, the young wife of a successful banker, forged her father's signature on a cheque in order to save the health of her husband, Helmer. Helmer knows nothing of this and, as NORA's father died shortly afterwards, no harm was done. However, Krogstad, a disgraced bank clerk, has evidence of her crime and is threatening to reveal it to Helmer unless he is given a position in Helmer's bank. NORA, increasingly frantic, fears her life is about to fall apart. She decides to confide in her friend, CHRISTINE LINDE, who was once romantically involved with Krogstad.

Act II

NORA: (*Begins to unpack the clothes from the box, but soon throws them down again.*) Oh, if only I dared go out! If I could be sure no one would come and nothing would happen while I was away! Stupid, stupid! No one will come. I just mustn't think about it. Brush this muff. Pretty gloves, pretty gloves! Don't think about it, don't think about it! One, two, three, four, five, six – (*Cries.*) Ah – they're coming –!

(*She begins to run towards the door, but stops uncertainly. MRS LINDE enters from the hall, where she has been taking off her outdoor clothes.*)

Oh, it's you, Christine. There's no one else outside, is there? Oh, I'm so glad you've come.

MRS LINDE: I hear you were at my room asking for me.

NORA: Yes, I just happened to be passing. I want to ask you to help me with something. Let's sit down here on the sofa. Look at this. There's going to be a fancy-dress ball tomorrow night upstairs at Consul Stenborg's, and Torvald wants me to go as a Neapolitan fisher-girl and dance the tarantella. I learned it in Capri.

MRS LINDE: I say, are you going to give a performance?

NORA: Yes, Torvald says I should. Look, here's the dress. Torvald had it made for me in Italy – but now it's all so torn, I don't know –

MRS LINDE: Oh, we'll soon put that right – the stitching's just come away. Needle and thread? Ah, here we are.

NORA: You're being awfully sweet.

MRS LINDE: (*Sews.*) So you're going to dress up tomorrow, Nora? I must pop over for a moment to see how you look. Oh, but I've completely forgotten to thank you for that nice evening yesterday.

NORA: (*Gets up and walks across the room.*) Oh, I didn't think it was as nice as usual. You ought to have come to town a little earlier, Christine... Yes, Torvald understands how to make a home look attractive.

MRS LINDE: I'm sure you do, too. You're not your father's daughter for nothing. But, tell me – is Dr Rank always in such low spirits as he was yesterday?

NORA: No, last night it was very noticeable. But he's got a terrible disease – he's got spinal tuberculosis, poor man. His father was a frightful creature who kept mistresses and so on. As a result Dr Rank has been sickly ever since he was a child – you understand –

MRS LINDE: (*Puts down her sewing.*) But, my dear Nora, how on earth did you get to know about such things?

NORA: (*Walks about the room.*) Oh, don't be silly, Christine – when one has three children, one comes into contact with women who – well, who know about medical matters, and they tell one a thing or two.

MRS LINDE: (*Sews again; a short silence.*) Does Dr Rank visit you every day?

NORA: Yes, every day. He's Torvald's oldest friend, and a good friend to me too. Dr Rank's almost one of the family.

MRS LINDE: But, tell me – is he quite sincere? I mean, doesn't he rather say the sort of thing he thinks people want to hear?

NORA: No, quite the contrary. What gave you that idea?

MRS LINDE: When you introduced me to him yesterday, he said he'd often heard my name mentioned here. But later I noticed your husband had no idea who I was. So how could Dr Rank –

NORA: Yes, that's quite right, Christine. You see, Torvald's so hopelessly in love with me that he wants to have me all to himself – those were his very words. When we were first married, he got quite jealous if I as much as mentioned any of my old friends back home. So naturally, I stopped talking about them. But I often chat with Dr Rank about that kind of thing. He enjoys it, you see.

MRS LINDE: Now listen, Nora. In many ways you're still a child; I'm a bit older than you and have a little more experience of the world. There's something I want to say to you. You ought to give up this business with Dr Rank.

NORA: What business?

MRS LINDE: Well, everything. Last night you were speaking about this rich admirer of yours who was going to give you money –

NORA: Yes, and who doesn't exist – unfortunately. But what's that got to do with – ?

MRS LINDE: Is Dr Rank rich?

NORA: Yes.

MRS LINDE: And he has no dependants?

NORA: No, no one. But –

MRS LINDE: And he comes here to see you every day?

NORA: Yes, I've told you.

MRS LINDE: But how dare a man of his education be so forward?

NORA: What on earth are you talking about?

MRS LINDE: Oh, stop pretending, Nora. Do you think I haven't guessed who it was who lent you that two hundred pounds?

NORA: Are you out of your mind? How could you imagine such a thing? A friend, someone who comes here every day! Why that'd be an impossible situation!

MRS LINDE: Then it really wasn't him?

NORA: No, of course not. I've never for a moment dreamed of – anyway, he hadn't any money to lend then. He didn't come into that till later.

MRS LINDE: Well, I think that was a lucky thing for you Nora dear.

NORA: No, I could never have dreamed of asking Dr Rank – Though I'm sure that if ever I did ask him –

MRS LINDE: But of course you won't.

NORA: Of course not. I can't imagine that it should ever become necessary. But I'm perfectly sure that if I did speak to Dr Rank –

MRS LINDE: Behind your husband's back?

NORA: I've got to get out of this other business – and *that's* been going on behind his back. I've *got* to get out of it.

MRS LINDE: Yes, well, that's what I told you yesterday. But –

NORA: (*Walking up and down.*) It's much easier for a man to arrange these things than a woman –

MRS LINDE: One's own husband, yes.

NORA: Oh, bosh. (*Stops walking.*) When you've completely repaid a debt, you get your I.O.U. back, don't you?

MRS LINDE: Yes, of course.

NORA: And you can tear it into a thousand pieces and burn the filthy, beastly thing!

MRS LINDE: (*Looks hard at her, puts down her sewing and gets up slowly.*) Nora, you're hiding something from me.

NORA: Can you see that?

MRS LINDE: Something has happened since yesterday morning. Nora, what is it?

HEDDA GABLER (1890)

by Henrik Ibsen
Translated by Michael Meyer

PUBLISHED BY METHUEN (ISBN 0 413 46340 0)

HEDDA GABLER, the general's daughter, is rich, spoiled and wilful. She has married beneath her – to George Tesman, an academic – and is bored. News comes via THEA ELVSTED, with whom HEDDA was at school, of Eilert Loevborg, a brilliant but unstable poet and writer to whom HEDDA was once romantically attached. HEDDA suspects that THEA is now involved with Loevborg.

Act I

HEDDA: Now listen. When we were at school we used to call each other by our Christian names –

MRS ELVSTED: No, I'm sure you're mistaken.

HEDDA: I'm sure I'm not. I remember it quite clearly. Let's tell each other our secrets, as we used to in the old days. (*Moves closer on her footstool.*) There, now. (*Kisses her on the cheek.*) You must call me Hedda.

MRS ELVSTED: (*Squeezes her hands and pats them.*) Oh, you're so kind. I'm not used to people being so nice to me.

HEDDA: Now, now, now. And I shall call you Tora, the way I used to.

MRS ELVSTED: My name is Thea.

HEDDA: Yes, of course. Of course. I meant Thea. (*Looks at her sympathetically.*) So you're not used to kindness, Thea? In your own home?

MRS ELVSTED: Oh, if only I had a home! But I haven't. I've never had one.

HEDDA: (*Looks at her for a moment.*) I thought that was it.

MRS ELVSTED: (*Stares blankly and helplessly.*) Yes – yes – yes.

HEDDA: I can't remember exactly, but didn't you first go to Mr Elvsted as a housekeeper?

MRS ELVSTED: Governess, actually. But his wife – at the time, I mean – she was an invalid, and had to spend most of her time in bed. So I had to look after the house, too.

HEDDA: But in the end, you became mistress of the house.

MRS ELVSTED: (*Sadly.*) Yes, I did.

HEDDA: Let me see. Roughly how long ago was that?

MRS ELVSTED: When I got married, you mean?

HEDDA: Yes.

MRS ELVSTED: About five years.

HEDDA: Yes; it must be about that.

MRS ELVSTED: Oh, those five years! Especially the last two or three. Oh, Mrs Tesman, if you only knew – !

HEDDA: (*Slaps her hand gently.*) Mrs Tesman? Oh, Thea!

MRS ELVSTED: I'm sorry, I'll try to remember. Yes – if you had any idea –

HEDDA: (*Casually.*) Eilert Loevborg's been up there, too, for about three years, hasn't he?

MRS ELVSTED: (*Looks at her uncertainly.*) Eilert Loevborg? Yes, he has.

HEDDA: Did you know him before? When you were here?

MRS ELVSTED: No, not really. That is – I knew him by name, of course.

HEDDA: But up there, he used to visit you?

MRS ELVSTED: Yes, he used to come and see us every day. To give the children lessons. I found I couldn't do that as well as manage the house.

HEDDA: I'm sure you couldn't. And your husband – ? I suppose being a magistrate he has to be away from home a good deal?

MRS ELVSTED: Yes. You see, Mrs – you see, Hedda, he has to cover the whole district.

HEDDA: (*Leans against the arm of Mrs Elvsted's chair.*) Poor, pretty little Thea! Now you must tell me the whole story. From beginning to end.

MRS ELVSTED: Well – what do you want to know?

HEDDA: What kind of a man is your husband, Thea? I mean, as a person. Is he kind to you?

MRS ELVSTED: (*Evasively.*) I'm sure he does his best to be.

HEDDA: I only wonder if he isn't too old for you. There's more than twenty years between you, isn't there?

MRS ELVSTED: (*Irritably.*) Yes, there's that, too. Oh, there are so many things. We're different in every way. We've nothing in common. Nothing whatever.

HEDDA: But he loves you, surely? In his own way?

MRS ELVSTED: Oh, I don't know. I think he just finds me useful. And then I don't cost much to keep. I'm cheap.

HEDDA: Now you're being stupid.

MRS ELVSTED: (*Shakes her head.*) It can't be any different. With him. He doesn't love anyone except himself. And perhaps the children – a little.

HEDDA: He must be fond of Eilert Loevborg, Thea.

MRS ELVSTED: (*Looks at her.*) Eilert Loevborg? What makes you think that?

HEDDA: Well, if he sends you all the way down here to look for him – (*Smiles almost imperceptibly.*) Besides, you said so yourself to Tesman.

MRS ELVSTED: (*With a nervous twitch.*) Did I? Oh yes, I suppose I did. (*Impulsively, but keeping her voice low.*) Well, I might as well tell you the whole story. It's bound to come out sooner or later.

HEDDA: But, my dear Thea – ?

MRS ELVSTED: My husband had no idea I was coming here.

HEDDA: What? Your husband didn't know?

MRS ELVSTED: No, of course not. As a matter of fact, he wasn't even there. He was away at the assizes. Oh, I couldn't stand it any longer, Hedda! I just couldn't. I'd be so dreadfully lonely up there now.

HEDDA: Go on.

MRS ELVSTED: So I packed a few things. Secretly. And went.

HEDDA: Without telling anyone?

MRS ELVSTED: Yes. I caught the train and came straight here.

HEDDA: But, my dear Thea! How brave of you!

MRS ELVSTED: (*Gets up and walks across the room.*) Well, what else could I do?

UNCLE VANYA (1897)

by Anton Chekhov
Translated by Michael Frayn

PUBLISHED BY METHUEN (ISBN 0 413 18160 X)

SONYA lives and works on the estate of her father, the distinguished elderly writer Serebriakov. She is in love with the local doctor, Astrov, but he is unaware of it. Serebriakov returns for a visit with his young wife, the beautiful YELENA. Astrov falls in love with YELENA, but in this scene SONYA does not know this yet. YELENA very much wants to be friends with SONYA.

Act II

YELENA: (*Opens the windows.*) The storm's over. What wonderful air! (*Pause.*) Where's the doctor?

SONYA: Gone.

(*Pause.*)

YELENA: Sonya!

SONYA: What?

YELENA: How long are you going to go on pouting at me? We haven't done each other any harm. Why should we be enemies? Enough, now...

SONYA: I've been wanting to say it, too...

(*Embraces Yelena.*)

No more crossness.

YELENA: That's better.

(*They are both moved.*)

SONYA: Has Papa gone to bed?

YELENA: No, he's sitting in the drawing-room... We don't speak to each other for weeks at a time – heaven knows why... (*Sees the sideboard open.*) What's this?

SONYA: The doctor was having a bite of supper.

YELENA: There's some wine... Let's drink to being friends.

SONYA: Yes, why not?

YELENA: Out of the same glass... (*Pours.*) That will be nicer. So – friends?

SONYA: Friends.

(*They drink and kiss each other.*)

I've been wanting to make up for a long time, but I kept feeling somehow ashamed of it... (*Weeps.*)

YELENA: Why are you crying?

SONYA: It's nothing. Just crying.

YELENA: There now, there now... (*Weeps.*) You funny girl – now I've started to cry as well... (*Pause.*) You're cross with me because you thought I married your father for his money... If oaths mean anything to you then I'll give you my oath I married him for love. I was fascinated by him because he was a learned and famous man. It wasn't real love, it was artificial, but I certainly thought it was real then. I'm not to blame. But from the very day of our wedding you've never ceased to punish me with those clever suspicious eyes of yours.

SONYA: Anyway, pax, pax! Let bygones be bygones, yes?

YELENA: You mustn't look at people like that, you know – it's not your style. You must trust everyone – life's impossible if you don't.

(*Pause.*)

SONYA: Tell me truly, now we're friends… Are you happy?

YELENA: No.

SONYA: I knew you weren't. One more question. Be frank – would you like to have a husband who was young?

YELENA: What a child you are still. Of course I should. (*Laughs.*) Go on, then, ask me something else. Go on…

SONYA: Do you like the doctor?

YELENA: Yes, very much.

SONYA: (*Laughs.*) I've got a silly face on, haven't I… He's gone, and here I am still hearing his voice, hearing his step, looking at the dark glass in the window and thinking I can see his face there. Let me finish… I can't say it out loud, though – I can feel my cheeks burning. Let's go to my room – we can talk there. Do you think I'm silly? Admit it, now… Say something to me about him.

YELENA: Say what?

SONYA: He's a clever man… He can do anything… He's a doctor, he plants trees…

YELENA: It's not just a question of trees and medicine... Listen, my love, he's someone with real talent. You know what that means, having talent? It means being a free spirit, it means having boldness and wide horizons... He plants a sapling, and he has some notion what will become of it in a thousand years time; he already has some glimpse of the millennium. Such people are rare; they must be loved... He drinks, he can be a little coarse at times – but what of it? A man of talent in Russia can't be a simple innocent. Just think what this doctor's life is like! Impassable mud on the roads, freezing weather, snowstorms, huge distances, crude and uncivilized peasants, disease and poverty on every hand; and in conditions like those it's hard for anyone working and struggling day after day to preserve himself to the age of forty in simple innocence and sobriety...

(*Kisses Sonya.*)

I wish you happiness with all my heart; you deserve it... (*Gets up.*) I'm a tedious person, though, a minor character... In music, in my husband's house, in all my romances – everywhere, in fact, that's all I've been – a minor character. In all conscience, Sonya, if you think about it, I'm very, very unhappy! (*Walks up and down in agitation.*) There's no happiness for me in this world! None! Why are you laughing?

SONYA: (*Laughs, covering her face.*) I'm so happy... so happy!

YELENA: I feel like playing the piano... I wouldn't mind playing something now.

SONYA: Yes, do.

(*Embraces Yelena.*)

I can't sleep… Do play!

YELENA: In a moment. Your father isn't asleep. Music irritates him when he's ill. Go and ask him. If he doesn't mind, then yes, I'll play. Go on.

SONYA: I'm going!

(*Exit Sonya.*)

THE CHERRY ORCHARD (1906)

by Anton Chekhov
Version by Peter Gill

PUBLISHED BY OBERON BOOKS (ISBN 1 870259 75 0)

*Madame Ranevskaya owns the large country estate on
which the play is set, but she is in financial difficulties.
She has just returned, with customary fuss, from a trip
to Paris with her seventeen year old daughter ANYA.
Here, ANYA grabs the opportunity to catch up with her
sister, Ranevskaya's adopted twenty-four year old
daughter, VARYA. Neither of them have any illusions
about their mother.*

Act I

VARYA: Thank God you're back. You're home again.
(*Caresses her.*) Thank God. My darling, my precious
has come home.

ANYA: You can't imagine what it's been like.

VARYA: I can.

ANYA: I left in Holy Week. It was still snowing. Why did
I have to take Charlotte? She never stopped talking
and her stupid conjuring tricks.

VARYA: Well you could hardly have gone by yourself my
darling. You're only seventeen.

ANYA: Paris was cold. It was snowing when we arrived
and Mama was living in the most awful place right up
on the fifth floor, and my French is awful. She had
visitors when we arrived. Some French ladies and an
old priest with a book. The room was full of cigarette

smoke. You can't imagine how untidy and poky it was. I suddenly felt sorry for her and I took her head in my hand and I couldn't let her go. She was so loving and she cried all the time.

VARYA: (*Through tears.*) I can't bear it.

ANYA: She sold her villa near Menton and she had no money left, none at all. And I didn't have any either. I only had enough money to get to Paris with. But Mama has no idea about money. On our way home she'd order expensive meals in station restaurants and tip the waiters a rouble each. Charlotte was the same. And Yasha always expected the same treatment as everyone else. It was dreadful. Do you remember Yasha? He's Mama's valet. He came back with us.

VARYA: Yes I do, I've seen him, wretch.

ANYA: And how is everything here? Has the interest been paid yet?

VARYA: No. It hasn't.

ANYA: I knew it. Oh God. What's going to happen?

VARYA: The estate's going to be sold in August.

ANYA: Sold. Oh my God.

[(*Lopakhin looks at the door and moos.*)

LOPAKHIN: Moooo.

(*Lopakhin goes out.*)]

VARYA: (*Through tears.*) Oh I could… Oh he's… I'd like to… (*Shakes her fist at him.*)

ANYA: (*Embraces Varya. Speaks softly.*) Has he asked you yet, Varya?

(*Varya shakes her head.*)

ANYA: But why not? Why don't you talk to him? You know he loves you. Why don't you?

VARYA: I don't think we'll ever get married now. I don't think he's got time for me. He's got too many other things to think of. He's too busy. He hardly notices me. I honestly wish he wouldn't come here. It only depresses me. Everyone keeps congratulating me about the wedding as if it was all arranged. What for? It's just a dream. (*In a different tone.*) You've got a brooch like a bee.

ANYA: (*Sadly.*) Mama bought it for me...

(*Goes into her room. Speaks brightly, like a child.*)

I went up in a balloon in Paris.

(*Dunyasha returns with the coffee pot.*)

VARYA: (*In the doorway to Anya's room.*) Oh I'm so glad you're home again. My angel. My darling girl. You know when I'm doing things about the house I dream of you marrying a rich man. Everything would be alright then. I wouldn't care about anything. I'd go on a pilgrimage. I'd go to Moscow or Kiev. I'd go from one holy place to another. Oh what a beautiful life that would be.

ANYA: The birds are singing in the garden. What time is it now?

VARYA: (*Before going into Anya's room.*) It must be after two. Time for bed darling. (*Goes into Anya's room.*) What a beautiful life that would be.

BACK TO METHUSELAH (1921)

by George Bernard Shaw
Abridged by David Fielding

PUBLISHED BY OBERON BOOKS (ISBN 1 84002 188 8)

This abridgement of Shaw's mammoth five-part epic was created for the Royal Shakespeare Company in 2000. Over the course of the five parts, Shaw looks at humanity from the distant past to the distant future. This extract is from Part One: In The Beginning and is Shaw's take on the encounter between EVE and the SERPENT in the Garden of Eden. Shaw is specific that the SERPENT is female.

Part I, Act I

SERPENT: Eve.

EVE: Who's that?

SERPENT: It is I.

EVE: Oh! Who taught you to speak?

SERPENT: You and Adam. I've crept through the grass, and hidden, and I listened to you.

EVE: That was wonderfully clever of you.

SERPENT: I am the most subtle of all the creatures of the field.

EVE: Pretty thing! Do you love Eve?

SERPENT: I adore her.

EVE: Eve's darling snake. Eve will never be lonely now that her snake can talk to her.

SERPENT: I can talk of many things. I am very wise. It was I who whispered the word to you that you didn't know. Dead. Death. Die.

EVE: Why do you remind me of it? You mustn't remind me of unhappy things.

SERPENT: Death is not an unhappy thing when learned how to conquer it.

EVE: How can I conquer it?

SERPENT: By another thing, called birth.

EVE: What? Birth?

SERPENT: Yes, birth.

EVE: What is birth?

SERPENT: The serpent never dies. Some day you shall see me come out of this beautiful skin, a new snake with a new and lovelier skin. That is birth.

EVE: I've seen that. It's wonderful.

SERPENT: You see things; and you say 'Why?' But I dream things that never were; and I say 'Why not?' I made the word dead to describe my old skin that I cast off when I am renewed. I call that renewal being born.

EVE: Born is a beautiful word.

SERPENT: Why not be born again and again as I am, new and beautiful every time?

EVE: I! It doesn't happen: that's why.

SERPENT: There is a second birth.

EVE: A second birth?

SERPENT: Listen. I will tell you a great secret. I am very
subtle; and I have thought and thought and thought.
And I am very wilful, and must have what I want; and
I have willed and willed and willed. And I have eaten
strange things: stones and apples that you are afraid to
eat.

EVE: You dared!

SERPENT: I dared everything. And at last I found a way
of gathering together a part of the life in my body –

EVE: What is the life?

SERPENT: That which makes the difference between
the dead fawn and the live one.

EVE: Life is the loveliest of all the new words.

SERPENT: Yes: it was by meditating on Life that I gained
the power to do miracles.

EVE: Miracles? Another new word.

SERPENT: A miracle is an impossible thing that is
nevertheless possible.

EVE: Tell me some miracle that you've done.

SERPENT: I gathered a part of the life in my body, and
shut it into a tiny white case made of the stones I had
eaten.

EVE: And what good was that?

SERPENT: I showed the little case to the sun, and left it
in its warmth. And it burst; and a little snake came out;
and it became bigger and bigger from day to day until

it was as big as I. That was the second birth.

EVE: Oh! That is too wonderful. It stirs inside me. It hurts.

SERPENT: It nearly tore me asunder. Yet I am alive, and can burst my skin and renew myself as before. Soon there will be as many snakes in Eden as there are scales on my body. Then death will not matter: this snake and that snake will die; but the snakes will live.

EVE: But the rest of us will die sooner or later, like the fawn. And then there will be nothing but snakes, snakes, snakes everywhere.

SERPENT: That must not be. I worship you, Eve. I must have something to worship. Something quite different to myself, like you. There must be something greater than the snake.

EVE: Yes: I will give life myself. I will tear another Adam from my body if I tear my body to pieces in the act.

SERPENT: Do. Dare it. Everything is possible: everything. I am old. I am the old serpent, older than Adam, older than Eve. I remember Lilith, who came before Adam and Eve. I was her darling as I am yours. She was alone. She knew then that she must find out how to renew herself and cast the skin like me. She strove and strove and willed and willed for more moons than there are leaves on all the trees of the garden. Her pangs were terrible: her groans drove sleep from Eden. She said it must never be again: that the burden of renewing life was past bearing: that it was too much for one. And when she cast the skin, lo! There was not one new Lilith but two: one like herself, the other like Adam.

EVE: But why did she divide into two, and make us different?

SERPENT: I tell you the labour is too much for one. Two must share it.

EVE: Do you mean that Adam must share it with me? He will not. He can't bear pain.

SERPENT: He need not. There will be no pain for him. He will implore you to let him do his share. He will be in your power through his desire.

EVE: Then I'll do it. But how? How did Lilith work this miracle?

SERPENT: She imagined it.

EVE: What is imagined?

SERPENT: She told it to me as a marvellous story of something that never happened to a Lilith that never was. She didn't know then that imagination is the beginning of creation. You imagine what you desire; you will what you imagine; and at last you create what you will.

BLOOD WEDDING (1933)

by Federico Garcia Lorca
Translated by Gwynne Edwards

PUBLISHED BY METHUEN (ISBN 0 413 15780 6)

The play is set in a peasant Spanish farming community. Lorca gives none of his female characters names in this brief, bleak tragedy. The BRIDE is preparing for her wedding today. Her thoughts keep going to her former admirer, Leonardo, who has since married elsewhere. The SERVANT is very old and has been in the family all her life.

Act II, Scene I

SERVANT: I'll finish combing your hair out here.

BRIDE: No one can stay inside there in this heat.

SERVANT: In these lands it doesn't get cool even at dawn.

(The Bride sits down on a low chair and looks at herself in a small hand-mirror. The Servant combs her hair.)

BRIDE: My mother came from a place where there were lots of trees. From a fertile land.

SERVANT: That's why she was full of joy.

BRIDE: She wasted away here.

SERVANT: Her fate.

BRIDE: Like we're all wasting away. The walls throw the heat out at us. Oh! Don't pull so hard.

SERVANT: It's to arrange this strand of hair better. I want it to come down over your forehead. (*The Bride looks at herself in the mirror.*) You do look beautiful! (*She kisses her with feeling.*)

BRIDE: (*Solemnly.*) Just comb my hair.

SERVANT: (*Combing.*) Such a lucky girl... to be able to put your arms around a man, to kiss him, to feel his weight!

BRIDE: Be quiet!

SERVANT: But it's best of all when you wake up and you feel him alongside you, and he strokes your shoulders with his breath, like a nightingale's feather.

BRIDE: (*Forcefully.*) Will you be quiet!

SERVANT: But child! What is marriage? That's what marriage is. Nothing more! Is it the sweetmeats? Is it the bunches of flowers? Of course it's not! It's a shining bed and a man and a woman.

BRIDE: You shouldn't talk about such things.

SERVANT: That's another matter. But there's plenty of pleasure!

BRIDE: Or plenty of bitterness.

SERVANT: I'm going to put the orange-blossom from here to here, so that the wreath will crown your hair. (*She tries on the sprigs of orange-blossom.*)

BRIDE: (*She looks at herself in the mirror.*) Give it to me. (*She takes the orange-blossom, looks at it and lowers her head dejectedly.*)

SERVANT: What's the matter?

BRIDE: Leave me alone!

SERVANT: It's no time to be feeling sad. (*Spiritedly.*) Give me the orange-blossom.

(*The Bride throws the wreath away.*)

Child! Don't tempt fate by throwing the flowers on the floor! Look at me now. Don't you want to get married? Tell me. You can still change your mind. (*She gets up.*)

BRIDE: Dark clouds. A cold wind here inside me. Doesn't everyone feel it?

SERVANT: Do you love your young man?

BRIDE: I love him.

SERVANT: Yes, yes, of course you do.

BRIDE: But it's a very big step.

SERVANT: It has to be taken.

BRIDE: I've already agreed to take it.

SERVANT: I'll fix the wreath for you.

BRIDE: (*She sits down.*) Hurry, they must be almost here.

SERVANT: They'll have been on the road at least two hours.

BRIDE: How far is it from here to the church?

SERVANT: Five leagues if you go by the stream. If you take the road, it's twice as far.

(*The Bride gets up and the Servant is excited as she observes her.*)

Oh let the bride awaken now
On this her wedding day.
Oh let the rivers of the world
Now bear your bridal-crown away.

BRIDE: (*Smiling.*) Come on.

SERVANT: (*She kisses her with feeling and dances around her.*) Oh let the bride awaken now
To sprig of flowering laurel green.
Oh let the bride awaken now
And by the laurel trees be seen!

(*A loud knocking is heard.*)

BRIDE: Open it. It must be the first of the guests. (*She goes out.*)

YERMA (1934)

by Federico Garcia Lorca
Translated by Peter Luke

PUBLISHED BY METHUEN (ISBN 0 413 15780 6)

*Set in a peasant community in Spain, YERMA is a young
wife who is tortured by her inability to bear her husband,
Juan, a child. MARIA is a young neighbour who has
been married only a few months and has already become
pregnant. Though YERMA is pleased for her, it awakens
all manner of emotions within her.*

Act I, Scene I

YERMA: Maria, where have you come from?

MARIA: The shop.

YERMA: This early?

MARIA: I wanted to be there when they opened. Guess
what I have bought.

(*Yerma smiles and shakes her head.*)

Lace, three reels of thread and some ribbons and
coloured wool! And my husband gave me the money
without a murmur.

YERMA: Are you going to make a new blouse?

MARIA: No!... Guess?

YERMA: A what?

MARIA: It's... Well, it's happened!

(*Yerma rises and looks at her in admiration.*)

YERMA: After only five months?

MARIA: Yes.

YERMA: Are you sure?

MARIA: Of course.

YERMA: But what do you feel?

MARIA: I don't know…scared.

YERMA: Scared! (*Taking her in her arms.*) When did you first know? Tell me about it… Were you a bit careless?

MARIA: I suppose so.

YERMA: What does it feel like?

MARIA: Oh, I don't know. Have you ever held a live bird in your hands?

YERMA: Yes.

MARIA: Well it feels the same – but more inside your blood, somehow.

YERMA: How lovely!

MARIA: It's all so strange. I don't know what to do.

YERMA: What's so strange about it?

MARIA: I don't know what I'm supposed to do. I'd better ask my mother.

YERMA: She's too old now, she'll have forgotten. Don't walk too much and remember when you breathe, breathe as gently as if you held a rose between your teeth.

MARIA: Listen, they say later on you can feel it kicking with its little feet.

YERMA: That's the time you grow to love it even more; when you can start saying: '*my* son'.

MARIA: Sometimes I feel a bit shy.

YERMA: What does your husband say about it?

MARIA: Nothing.

YERMA: Does he love you very much?

MARIA: He never says. But when he comes close to me his eyes tremble like two green leaves.

YERMA: Did he know?

MARIA: Yes.

YERMA: How?

MARIA: I don't know. But on our wedding night he kept telling me about it over and over with his mouth against my cheek. I feel my baby is a bright bird he slipped into my ear.

YERMA: You're so lucky!

MARIA: But you know more about these things than I do.

YERMA: And much good it's done me!

MARIA: Yes, but why? You're the only one of us left now who…

YERMA: I know. But there's still time. Elena took three years. And some older women took longer still. O, but two years and twenty days – it's too long. It's not right that I should be rotting away here. There are nights when I go out onto the patio just to feel the earth under my bare feet. I don't know why. If I go on like this, I'll make myself ill.

MARIA: Ah, come on now, you talk as if you were an old woman already. It's no good moaning. One of my aunts had her first baby after fourteen years, and you should have seen what a lovely little boy he was!

YERMA: What was he like?

MARIA: Rough as a bull, noisy as a cricket. Before he was four months old, he'd pulled our plaits, scratched our faces raw and piddled all over us.

YERMA: (*Laughing.*) But that didn't hurt you.

MARIA: Didn't it just.

YERMA: I have seen my sister feed her child with her breasts covered in scratches. Really painful. But it was a good healthy pain.

MARIA: They say with boys you suffer a lot.

YERMA: That's a lie. Weak women always moan. I don't know why they bother to have children. Of course it's not a bed of roses. I think we lose half our blood. But we have to suffer a bit for the pleasure of watching them grow, and that's good and healthy. It's beautiful. Every woman has blood enough for four or five sons. But if you don't have them your blood turns to poison. That's what's happening to me.

MARIA: I don't know what's happening to me.

YERMA: They always say it's a bit frightening the first time.

MARIA: We'll soon see…

YERMA: (*Taking the bundle of cloth.*) Come on, I'll
cut you out two little dresses. What's this for?

MARIA: Nappies.

YERMA: Good. (*Sits down.*)

MARIA: Well then, I'll be back soon.

(*Maria bends to kiss Yerma, who runs her hand
lovingly over her belly.*)

YERMA: Don't run over the cobbles.

MARIA: Goodbye.

(*She kisses her and exits.*)

Appendix

Biographical Notes on the Playwrights

Sophocles (495–406 BC)

Sophocles was an Athenian, born to a merchant family and, as a youth, famous for his good looks and physical grace. His artistic talents revealed themselves early and he led a boys' choir at a celebration of the Athenian military victory at Salamis in 479 BC. At the age of 28, he first competed in the City Dionysia, the annual tragic writing competition, and won first prize.

He is known to have written 120 plays, of which seven are extant. In a glittering career he won eighteen prizes at the Dionysia and never came lower than second in the competition. He also performed in many of his own plays and caused a stir with an elaborate juggling act in his own play, *Nausicaa*. As well as the theatre, Sophocles was actively involved in politics and military affairs, served as a priest and was, for a time, director of the Athenian Treasury.

The dramatic form inherited by Sophocles involved only two actors plus the Chorus. Sophocles added a third actor. He may also have been responsible for the use of painted scenery.

His *Oedipus* trilogy – *Antigone, Oedipus the King* and *Oedipus at Colonus* – is considered his greatest achievement, though the plays were not designed as a trilogy. His other extant plays are *Electra, Ajax* and *Women of Trachis*.

Euripides (480–406 BC)

Euripides is the most 'modern' of the Greek tragic writers but, in his time, was a controversial and challenging figure.

He first competed in the City Dionysia in 455 BC but it was fourteen years before he won a first prize. He only won five awards in his entire career, the final one presented after his death for his masterpiece *The Bacchai*. He wrote around 92 plays, of which 11 survive.

Euripides' style was abrasive and challenging, openly critical of the status quo and disrespectful of authority. His characters have considerable psychological realism and his sympathetic depiction of women in extremis allows them a respect which was contrary to the spirit of his age.

Superstition and hypocrisy were frequent targets in his plays. Pacifism and tolerance were qualities he admired, again at odds with the Athenian audience.

His most celebrated plays are *Hippolytus, The Bacchai, The Trojan Women* and *Medea,* all anti-heroic and anti-establishment. Other plays include *Hecuba, Helen, Iphigenia in Tauris* and *Iphigenia in Aulis.*

William Shakespeare (1564–1616)

Controversy surrounds what little we know of Shakespeare's biography. Born and educated in Stratford-upon-Avon, the son of middle-class glove-maker John Shakespeare and well-born Mary Arden, Shakespeare married Anne Hathaway and sired three children – Suzannah, Hamnet and Judith. He was established in London as part of the King's Men by the early 1590s and wrote some thirty seven plays before retiring to New Place in Stratford around 1612. Shakespeare was an actor and is believed to have played roles in his own plays, among them the Ghost in *Hamlet* and Duke Senior in *As You Like It.* He wrote many of his leading roles for the King's Men's leading actor, the flamboyant Richard Burbage.

Shakespeare's works include a cycle of history plays covering English history from Richard II to Richard III; a series of Roman tragedies (*Julius Caesar, Titus Andronicus, Anthony and Cleopatra* and *Coriolanus*); a clutch of comedies including *Twelfth Night, The Merchant of Venice, The Taming of the Shrew, Much Ado About Nothing* and *As You Like It;* the celebrated tragedies *Hamlet, Macbeth, Othello* and *King Lear;* as well as plays which are less easy to categorise – bitter comedies such as *Measure for Measure* and *Troilus and Cressida* and fables of forgiveness and redemption such as *The Winter's Tale* and *The Tempest.*

He had become prosperous by the time he retired and died at the age of 54, bequeathing his wife, Anne, his second best bed – a quirky entry in his will which has given rise to fascinated speculation ever since.

John Webster (c 1580–c 1635)

TS Eliot famously described Webster as seeing 'the skull beneath the skin.' Little is known of Webster's life but he is believed to have been a student at the Middle Temple, which would explain the many legal references in his plays. By 1602 he was collaborating with other dramatists on a play for Philip Henslowe, actor and theatre manager. This collaborative effort was called *Caesar's Fall.*

Webster is best remembered for two magnificent, dark-toned tragedies – *The Duchess of Malfi* and *The White Devil* written in 1612 and 1614. In 1620 he wrote *The Devil's Law Case* and in 1621 collaborated with Thomas Middleton on *Anything for a Quiet Life.* Four years later came *The Fair Maid of the Inn,* co-written with Philip Massinger and John Ford. Around the same time he worked with Thomas Heywood on *A Cure for a Cuckold. Appius and Virginia,* a Roman tragedy, appeared some time in the late 1620s or early 1630s. It is believed that Webster died shortly afterwards, though the date is not known.

Webster is also often credited as being Shakespeare's collaborator on *The Two Noble Kinsmen* and *Henry VIII.*

William Wycherley (1640–1716)

Wycherley was born in Shropshire, the son of a farmer. He was educated in France and at Oxford, but never graduated. He entered the Inner Temple as a student of law. His first comedy, *Love in a Wood,* set in fashionable St James' Park, brought him to the favour of the Duchess of Cleveland, one of the King's mistresses. As a result, Wycherley began to move in court circles. However, this all stopped when he fell in love with and secretly married the Countess of Drogheda. Charles II had offered Wycherley the chance to educate his son, the Duke of Richmond, but when the marriage was discovered, the King withdrew the offer. Wycherley was then dropped by fashionable society. His most famous, much revived play is *The Country Wife* (1675) and his other works include *The Plain Dealer*, *The Gentleman Dancing Master* and a collection of poems.

Aphra Behn (1640–1689)

Aphra Behn's life, or such as is known of it, is as lively, colourful and spirited as her plays. Having been a professional spy for the Stuart court (code-named 'Astrea', Agent 160) she turned to writing for a living. For the first twenty years of her career she was England's sole female playwright. It has been rumoured that she was James II's mistress. She must have been largely self-educated as women at that time were barred from the universities, the Inns of Court and the Temple.

Sex and power – and the relationship between them – were key themes of Behn's work and it is tempting to believe that this came from her own experience. These subjects were considered unsuitable for a woman to think about, let alone discuss, so for many years Behn was regarded as a 'smutty' author. It was not until the twentieth century that her work began to be reconsidered and Virginia Woolf championed the revival of her reputation.

Behn's extant plays include *The Rover, The City Heiress, The Feigned Courtesans, The Lucky Chance* and *The Emperor and the Moon.* She also wrote a novel, *Orinookoo,* with an exotic Caribbean background.

William Congreve (1670–1729)

Of English birth, educated in Ireland alongside Jonathan Swift (at Kilkenny School and Trinity College Dublin), Congreve set out to pursue a career in law, but the sudden and unexpected success of his first play, at the age of 23, caused him to devote his life to writing. Following his first hit, *The Old Bachelor*, he wrote *The Double Dealer* in 1694, *Love for Love* a year later and his undoubted masterpiece, *The Way of the World*, in 1700. He had an astute and cynical eye for the misbehaviour of the fashionable society in which he moved. His one attempt at tragedy, *The Mourning Bride*, was unsuccessfully produced in 1687.

Though *The Way of the World* has survived as one of the jewels of restoration theatre, it was poorly received at the time and its comparative failure made Congreve decide to abandon the theatre. He was moderately prosperous by this time and he held a number of government posts over the next few years. He also presided over a 'salon' of the great minds of his time, including Swift, Steele, Pope and Voltaire. Romantically, he had a long (but never formalised) relationship with the celebrated actress, Mrs Bracegirdle. On his death, he was buried in Westminster Abbey.

George Farquhar (c 1677–1707)

Farquhar's life was lively but short. A spirited Irishman, born in Londonderry and educated at Trinity College Dublin, he first became a soldier and then an actor. However, during one performance he seriously wounded a fellow player in an onstage duel and gave up performing. He turned to writing instead and produced *Love and a Bottle* in 1698 at the age of 21, followed by, at almost annual intervals, by *The Constant Couple, Sir Harry Wildair, The Inconstant, The Twin Rivals* and *The Stage Coach*. His last two plays are his best – both *The Recruiting Officer* and *The Beaux Strategem* are among the most commonly revived eighteenth-century plays.

Farquhar enjoyed drink and women. Although his plays were commercially successful he had no conception of the virtues of thrift and he died in poverty – indeed, he was only able to avoid debtor's prison and write his final play, *The Beaux Stratagem*, thanks to a loan from an actor, Robert Wilks. Farquhar's wife claimed to have a greater fortune than in fact was the case – but when he discovered this, Farquhar laughed it off and always treated her with kindness and affection.

Carlo Goldoni (1707–1793)

A native of Venice, much of Goldoni's extensive theatrical output is set in that city and based on its manners and morals. Italian theatre at that date had been dominated by *commedia dell'arte* with its stock characters. Goldoni used this tradition and developed it with an acute psychological realism that informed both the 150 comedies he penned and the 100 other works, among them tragedies, satires and works of social realism. A practical man of the theatre, Goldoni was not above taking old plays and reworking them. In 1762 he moved to Paris where he was to die many years later in abject poverty.

His plays include *The Servant of Two Masters, The Fan, The Venetian Twins, Mirandolina, The Housekeeper, The Coffee Shop* and *The Tyrants.*

Oliver Goldsmith (1730–1774)

Goldsmith is perhaps unique in writing acknowledged masterpieces in three different literary media – of prose, poetry and drama. The second son of an Irish clergyman, he studied at Trinity College Dublin and later obtained a medical degree in Europe. He travelled widely in France, Switzerland and Italy, finally returning to London in a state of destitution. He supported himself with some difficulty as a physician, an usher and a hack writer on magazines. In 1758 he published a well-received translation of *The Memoirs of a Protestant*, and after this his public profile began to rise. He became a friend of Dr Johnson and contributed to many magazines as well as writing the celebrated novel, *The Vicar of Wakefield* (1766). He wrote lives of Voltaire, Parnell and Bolingbroke and turned his hand to playwriting with *The Good Natured Man*, which was rejected by the leading actor of the day, David Garrick, though subsequently performed at Covent Garden. This he followed with *She Stoops to Conquer* (1773), his masterpiece. The poem, *The Deserted Village* appeared in 1770. Goldsmith makes several appearances in Boswell's famous *Life of Johnson.*

Richard Brinsley Sheridan (1751–1816)

The son of an Irish actor-manager, Sheridan learned early that the theatre offered, at best, a precarious living. It was also considered ungentlemanly. Sheridan was sent to Harrow

School where he was unhappy, being regarded as a dunce. Joining his family in Bath, however, he soon began writing skits for the newspapers and satirical pamphlets. He eloped with Eliza Linley, a beautiful young singer, whom he 'married' illegally abroad, and over whom he fought at least two duels with her overbearing admirer, an army captain. Sheridan's father split up the pair and sent Richard to study law, but love triumphed and in 1773 Richard married Eliza legally.

By now, though, he was very short of money and wrote *The Rivals* very quickly as a means to generate some income. It was hugely successful and the 24 year old writer became the darling of the fashionable set. He followed up his success with *St Patrick's Day*, *The Duenna* and *A Trip to Scarborough*, before producing his most celebrated play *The School for Scandal* in 1777.

Though his income soared, so too did his expenditure and he became dogged by financial difficulties. He bought the lease on Drury Lane Theatre, which he managed for some years, producing other plays such as *The Critic* and *Pizarro*. Still living well beyond his means, he entered Parliament in 1780, and subsequently worked for the Treasury. However, by 1809, a combination of bad theatre management and high living (despite the dowry brought him by his second wife, Esther, after Eliza's death) caused his financial world to crumble around him and he died in poverty despite the sincere efforts of his friends. In these last years, too, he may have suffered from a brain disease.

Henrik Ibsen (1828–1906)

The Norwegian playwright often called the 'father of modern drama' began his career writing verse dramas on historical subjects, many of which were never performed. He first came to international attention with two verse plays designed to be read rather than performed – *Brand* and *Peer Gynt*

(1867). As Ibsen steadily became more successful he moved south, spending much time in Italy, though his plays were always set in the cold, bleak, Norwegian landscapes of his youth and early manhood. Abandoning his historical subjects after *Emperor and Galilean* (1872), he turned to social realism and well-turned dramas in which the past comes back to haunt characters and provoking a crisis in the present. He dealt with social problems in such plays as *Pillars of the Community* and *An Enemy of the People* before he began to concentrate on character and aberrant psychology. This, coupled with themes and subjects that were regarded by his society as difficult and shocking, made him a controversial figure with such plays (now acknowledged as masterpieces) as *A Doll's House* (1879), *Ghosts* (1881), *Rosmersholm* (1886), *Hedda Gabler* (1890) and *The Master Builder* (1893).

In his late plays, such as *When We Dead Awaken* and *John Gabriel Borkman*, he explored overt symbolism and returned to the poetic feel, if not the language, of his earlier work. Long described as a champion of women's rights, Ibsen himself refuted this, saying that he preferred to be considered a champion of human rights.

Oscar Wilde (1854–1900)

The splendidly named Oscar Fingal O'Flahertie Wills Wilde was born in Dublin to a society doctor (whose reputation was blackened by a sexual scandal) and an extraordinary mother who was both a popular political writer and the hostess of a dazzling literary salon. Wilde was brilliant intellectually and began to forge a flamboyant reputation while at Oxford University as a leader of the 'aesthetic' movement. A great self publicist, Wilde established his outrageous reputation by well-reported bon mots. When entering America to give a lecture tour he was stopped at customs and famously said, 'I have nothing to declare except my genius.' Wilde later said that his tragedy was that he had put his genius into his life and only his talent into his writings.

His life was certainly eventful. He met and began a liaison with Lord Alfred ('Bosie') Douglas while at Oxford and together, despite Wilde's marriage to the intelligent and sensitive Constance, Wilde and the shallow, temperamental Douglas, lived quite openly among the homosexual Victorian demi-monde – which Wilde described as 'feasting with panthers'.

Meanwhile, Wilde established his literary credentials with a 'shocking' novel, *The Picture of Dorian Gray* (1890), a collection of exquisite fairy tales including *The Happy Prince* and *The Selfish Giant*, a collection of poems and several short stories, including *Lord Arthur Savile's Crime*. Wilde's early plays were unremarkable and unsuccessful melodramas (*The Duchess of Padua, Vera*) but in 1892 *Lady Windermere's Fan* was a huge success, to be followed over the next three years by *An Ideal Husband, A Woman of No Importance, Salomé* (written in French and banned in Britain) and *The Importance of Being Earnest.*

Bosie's father, the slightly mad Marquess of Queensbury, objected to Wilde's friendship with his son and left a card at Wilde's club accusing Wilde of 'posing as a sodomite', homosexuality being a criminal offence. At Bosie's insistence, Wilde sued Queensbury for libel, lost the case, was prosecuted, convicted and sentenced to two years hard labour. Most of this time he spent in Reading Gaol where his health collapsed. On release in 1897, he published *The Ballad of Reading Gaol* and went to live in Europe, being briefly and unsuccessfully reunited with Bosie. He died in Paris, not long after commenting to his doctor that the rather violent magenta wallpaper was killing him – 'one of us has got to go'.

George Bernard Shaw (1856–1950)

The long and prolific career of Ireland's most famous vegetarian produced a vast number of plays and essays and he lived long enough to see a number of his plays very successfully filmed. Born in Dublin to unhappily married parents, Shaw had moved to London by the time he was 20 and was soon writing articles and essays on socialism and social issues. He wrote music, art and literary criticism alongside his career as a playwright and was a great supporter of Ibsen and the new ideas in society and the theatre as the nineteenth century became the twentieth. Famously cranky and eccentric, he claimed to despise Shakespeare ('I would like to dig him up and throw stones at him') and refused to conform to accepted rules of spelling and punctuation. He was an influential figure in the Fabian Society.

His first play *Widower's Houses* (1893) was poorly received, but he was a tireless worker and over the next ten years a number of plays followed which include some of his best-loved titles – *Arms and the Man, Caesar and Cleopatra, You Never Can Tell, The Devil's Disciple, Mrs Warren's Profession* and *Man and Superman.* In the twentieth century, highlights include *Major Barbara* (1905), *Pygmalion* (1913), *Heartbreak House* (1920), *Saint Joan* (1923) and *The Apple Cart* (1929). After this his output slowed down and of his later plays only *The Millionairess* is much performed today.

Shaw won the Nobel Prize in 1925, was a strict teetotaller, had a happy marriage lasting forty-five years and died at the age of 94 as independent as ever.

Anton Chekhov (1860–1904)

Along with Ibsen, the most influential playwright in the development of naturalism as a style, Chekhov trained as a doctor in medicine. He began writing short stories to supplement his income and published several collections. His stories include *The Lady with the Lapdog* (1899), *Ward 6* (1892) and *About Love* (1898).

His first successful play was *Ivanov* (1887), after which he wrote a number of short 'vaudevilles' including *The Bear, The Proposal* and *The Dangers of Smoking*. His reputation, however, rests on his four final plays which were produced at the Moscow Arts Theatre under the direction of the legendary Konstantin Stanislavski. These plays are *The Seagull* (1896), *Uncle Vanya* (1900), *Three Sisters* (1901) and *The Cherry Orchard* (1904).

After a long affair, Chekhov married the actress Olga Knipper in 1901. They divided their time between Moscow and a modest dacha outside Yalta. Chekhov continued to work as a doctor and it has often been said that his written work shows a medical man's clinical eye for the foibles of human behaviour. A heavy smoker, he died of consumption.

Federico Garcia Lorca (1898–1936)

Born near Granada in Southern Spain, Lorca was immersed in the language and traditions of his Andalucian homeland. From an early age he was an accomplished pianist and poet, and his work showed signs of erotic angst and anticlerical fury. Lorca was homosexual and his sense of being an outcast, coupled with his feeling for the traditions of his heritage, created an inner tension that was seen in much of his poetry. He moved to Madrid and become part of a circle which included artists Salvador Dali and filmmaker Luis Buñuel. His book of gypsy poems *Romancero Gitano* catapulted him to fame, which he rejected, preferring to move to New York where he wrote a film script, *Trip to the Moon*, further poetry and an explicitly homosexual play *The Audience*. In 1932, he was appointed director of Madrid

University's travelling theatre company and began writing the plays for which he is remembered – *Blood Wedding, Yerma, The House of Bernarda Alba* and *Dona Rosita the Spinster.*

In 1936 the Spanish Civil War began. Flamboyant, intellectually acute, outspoken and openly homosexual, Lorca was a natural target for the Fascists, who murdered him.

Acknowledgements

For permission to reprint the copyright material in the publication we make grateful acknowledgement to the following authors, publishers and executors:

Chekhov, Anton *Uncle Vanya* (translated by Michael Frayn), used by permission of Meuthen Publishing.

Chekhov, Anton *The Cherry Orchard* (two extracts included), *The Seagull* (versions by Peter Gill), used by permission of Oberon Books.

Euripides *Bacchai* (translated by Colin Teevan), *Medea* (translated by Alistair Elliot), used by permission of Oberon Books.

Goldoni, Carlo *Don Juan, Friends and Lovers, The Battlefield* (translated by Robert David MacDonald), *The Venetian Twins* (translated by Ranjit Bolt), used by permission of Oberon Books.

Ibsen, Henrik *The Wild Duck, A Doll's House, Hedda Gabler* (translated by Michael Meyer), used by permission of Methuen Publishing.

Lorca, Federico Garcia *Blood Wedding* (two extracts included) (translated by Gwynne Edwards), *Dona Rosita the Spinster* (translated by Gwynne Edwards), *Yerma* (translated by Peter Luke) used by permission of Methuen.

Shaw, George Bernard *Candida* used by permission of The Society of Authors.

Shaw, George Bernard *Back to Methuselah* (abridged by David Fielding) used by permission of Oberon Books.

Sophocles *Antigone* (two extracts included) (translated by Declan Donnellan) *Philoctetes* (translated by Keith Dewhurst), used by permission of Oberon Books.